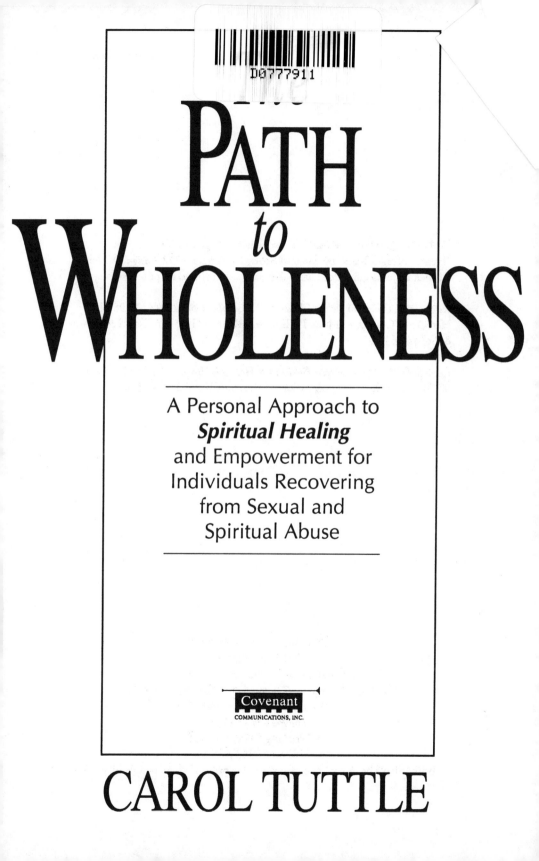

D0777911

# The

# PATH

# *to*

# WHOLENESS

A Personal Approach to
**Spiritual Healing**
and Empowerment for
Individuals Recovering
from Sexual and
Spiritual Abuse

Covenant
COMMUNICATIONS, INC.

# CAROL TUTTLE

# DEDICATION

To my husband Jon and my four beautiful children who
have supported me through the discovery and healing
of my painful past. Thank you for never giving up.

# ACKNOWLEDGEMENTS

The assistance and support of many people helped make this book possible:

My dear friend Betty, who spent countless hours on the phone with me going over the manuscript to make sure the content was right.

My sisters in CUC, who taught me how to come unto Christ on my path to wholeness. Thank you for listening, understanding, affirming, and offering unconditional love and support. Without your insights and examples I could not have written this book.

Chris Low, the editor of the *In Reflection* newsletter, who allowed me to quote survivors who had contributed to her publication.

Seymour Kessler, who taught me to believe in myself.

The survivors, who courageously shared their pain and reality with me because it would help others heal.

My editors, Julie Helm and Kerrill Sue Rollins, who both contributed their expertise to this project. And to Darla Hanks Isackson and Robby Nichols at Covenant Communications, thank you for believing that this book would make a difference and for working hard to make sure it could.

# CONTENTS

# PROLOGUE

*You must do the thing you think you cannot do.*
—*Eleanor Roosevelt*

Several years ago I was faced with the overwhelming and painful challenge of healing from child sexual abuse. I was raised in an active LDS family. We attended church regularly and our family gave the appearance that all was well. I attended Brigham Young University, earned my degree, and married in the LDS Temple. Once I had children, I left my job to stay home and be a full-time mother. I made choices that I hoped would bring me joy and happiness. After becoming a wife and mother, I became the classic "super woman" with the idea, "if I am good, life will be swell." I pushed hard to be the type of woman I thought I had to be. I became a perfectionist—someone who would take on too much and was always very busy. I was recognized as a "Family Leader of Tomorrow" and an "Outstanding Young Woman of America." By all appearances I looked nearly perfect. I heard frequently how well I did everything. I was the envy of others because my "doings" were so good. While staying home with small children, I also ran a small business, served as PTA president, and served in many church leadership positions. I planted beautiful flowers, grew a summer garden, cooked gourmet meals, sewed beautiful clothing for my children and *always* had a clean house.

That was my public side—my private side was very different. Through the years I started to decline emotionally. I struggled with eating disorders, bouts of low self-esteem, depression, and other trials, but always seemed to pull myself out. All those things seemed like ordinary challenges I could overcome, but after the birth of my fourth child, I really hit an emotional low. I went from a dysfunctional life to a nonfunctional one, where severe depression was the mood of the day. Rage and anger seeped in and burst open at inappropriate times, hurting me and my family on a regular basis. I had days when I could barely get out of my bed and see the day through. Trying to meet the needs of my family seemed overwhelming. I got to a point where I no longer wanted to go on living because life was too painful. I had never felt such darkness, despair, and confusion. I was serving others and "doing all the right things." Why was I suffering so? I spent many tearful anguishing moments on my knees seeking answers, asking my Heavenly Father for a release from this emotional pain. The answers began to come—I had never honestly dealt with the reality of my repeated child sexual abuse. I came to understand that my denial and addictions could no longer suppress the pain, shame, and worthlessness that festered within me. I knew that I had come to a point of decision—I must learn how to heal the wounds of my abusive past or allow them to destroy me, my marriage, and my family.

At the time of my greatest pain I felt, as Alma did, to cry from the depths of my soul: "O Jesus, thou Son of God, have mercy on me, who am in the gall of bitterness, and am encircled about by the everlasting chains of death" (Alma 36:18).

Through my commitment to heal I have come to feel as Jonah: "I cried by reason of mine affliction unto the Lord, and he heard me; out of the belly of hell cried I, and thou heardest my voice" (Jonah 2:2). As I have been blessed with the pure love of Christ, I have found ways to heal the tremendous pain of the abuse inflicted on me and to replace this pain with feelings of peace, harmony, empowerment, joy, and charity. In the prayerful quest for my own recovery, I have learned that coming unto Christ and living his gospel are critical in order to achieve a permanent and complete physical, emotional, and spiritual recovery. I have had the blessing of learning how to apply gospel tools and powers in order to heal. And though I am not a professional therapist, I have solidified my understanding of what it takes to heal from child sexual abuse.

During the healing process, I have re-experienced the wounds, the pain, and the needs—physical, emotional, and spiritual—that are unique to survivors with strong religious backgrounds. While there are a number of books and other publications that address how one can recover from childhood abuse, none are currently directed specifically to survivors who have a belief in God and who are struggling with their spiritual values and religious beliefs as a direct result of their abuse. I felt impressed to write this book in order to address that need.

It has been my experience that when the doctrines and powers of Christ's gospel are incorporated into the healing process, they offer the survivor a unique and empowering experience that can result in a full and complete recovery. For this reason, I have used throughout the book many scriptures from the Holy Bible as well as LDS scriptures from the Book of Mormon, the Doctrine and Covenants, and the Pearl of Great Price as resources for learning and reference.

In this book I have chosen to focus on myself and other women survivors who are members of the Church of Jesus Christ of Latter-day Saints (LDS or Mormon). We share the experience of child abuse that I know so profoundly, but we also share a belief in our Heavenly Father and in his son Jesus Christ who is our divine redeemer, as do all Christians.

Use this book as a guide, as you would any recovery book, choosing to draw from it what feels right for you. Each survivor's specific childhood trauma is different, resulting in a unique personal recovery experience. Be willing to put yourself first; healing requires a commitment of learning how to care for yourself and then choosing to act on that new-found knowledge.

If you are a survivor of incest or sexual abuse reading this book can help you realize that you too can overcome the pain of your past. If you are a survivor's friend, spouse, or parent, you will find insight that will enable you to help this special person recover.

If you were not sexually abused as a child but are recovering from other types of child abuse or trauma, or are dealing with current abuse, you will still find this book helpful. Whether you have been the victim of sexual, emotional, or physical abuse, alcoholic parents, divorce, mental illness, or the death of a loved one, recovery follows a similar course, and the same basic principles apply. I invite you to use this book as a healing tool.

My recovery has taught me that it is possible to take something that hurt me deeply and turn it around. My recovery has added a greater spiritual dimension to my life than all my other experiences combined. I now know and feel more than ever that I am a chosen daughter of my Heavenly Father.

Writing this book has offered me the chance to continue to heal and to gain deep spiritual insights through that healing. It has been a steady source of inspiration and amazement to me as the power and grace of God has been demonstrated through his son, Jesus Christ.

I hope you will allow the grace of God to come into your life. He will chase away the darkness as you do the work of healing, so you too will enjoy what has been promised to all of God's children—to understand through personal experience that "men [and women] are, that they might have joy" (2 Nephi 2:25).

# PART ONE
# THE PATH TO RECOVERY

# CHAPTER 1
## CHOOSING TO WALK THE PATH

*"What is REAL?" asked the Rabbit one day, when they were lying side by side near the nursery fender, before Nana came to tidy the room. "Does it mean having things that buzz inside you and a stick-out handle?"*

*"Real isn't how you are made," said the Skin Horse. "It's a thing that happens to you. When a child loves you for a long, long time, not just to play with, but REALLY loves you, then you become Real."*

*"Does it hurt?" asked the Rabbit.*

*"Sometimes," said the Skin Horse, for he was always truthful. "When you are Real you don't mind being hurt."*

*"Does it happen all at once, like being wound up," he asked, "or bit by bit?"*

*"It doesn't happen all at once," said the Skin Horse. "You become. It takes a long time. That's why it doesn't often happen to people who break easily, or have sharp edges, or who have to be carefully kept. Generally, by the time you are Real, most of your hair has been loved off, and your eyes drop out and you get loose in the joints and very shabby. But these things don't matter at all, because once you are Real*

*you can't be ugly, except to people who don't under-
stand."*

*"I suppose you are Real?" said the Rabbit, and
then he wished he had not said it, for he thought the
Skin Horse might be sensitive. But the Skin Horse
only smiled. "The Boy's Uncle made me Real," he
said. "That was a great many years ago; but once
you are Real you can't become unreal again. It lasts
for always."¹*

You may wonder if anyone can really recover from
incest and child sexual abuse. Can an individual live
a life free of the residual effects of this all-encompassing
childhood trauma and live with the freedom to make
choices as if the abuse never happened? Can such a person
ever feel a sense of self-worth free of feelings of abandonment, shame, and worthlessness? Can this same individual
enjoy the security of a trusting and unified relationship
with a spouse, participate in clear communication and true
intimacy, and enjoy through marriage the experience of
safe sexual and nonsexual physical companionship?

My answer to all of these questions is YES! Every survivor has the God-given right to heal. You or someone you
know can heal the wounds of incest and child sexual
abuse—although healing does require that you do a lot of
work and receive a lot of help. Remember always that
"with God all things are possible" (Mark 10:27). Most victims who choose not to get help find themselves adrift,
aimless, and desperate, tethered only to the secrets, the
shame, and the anger of the past.

The first step toward recovery is personal resolution.
This involves recognizing and accepting the reality that you
were sexually abused as a child. When you realize that you
can heal from these severe wounds and that you are, in fact,
responsible for taking care of yourself, then you can resolve

# The Inn
### AT
# JIM THORPE

DEAREST M,

PLEASE CONTINUE

TO LISTEN

∞,

M

24 Broadway • Jim Thorpe, PA 18229 • Phone: (717) 325-2599

to do whatever is necessary to make sure the healing takes place. The word *resolution* has a powerful meaning: "firmness of purpose, position arrived at after consideration, freedom from doubt or wavering, a quality of mind or temperament that enables one to stand fast in the face of opposition, hardship, or danger."[2]

As a survivor you are not responsible for the abuse you suffered as a child. But as an adult, you are responsible for taking care of yourself, for healing the wounds of oppression caused by your abuse. You have the God-given power within you to start the process of recovery by taking the second step—deciding to heal and to walk your path to wholeness.

According to an old Chinese saying, "Pure gold is not afraid of the refiner's fire." As a survivor of abuse you have not been free to feel your innate divine value or your worth of "pure gold." Your gold is there. It is just covered with an old, painted-on mask that you had to wear in order to live with the emotional scars and painful wounds that have not yet been healed. To get to your gold, you must remove the mask by burning it off: you must pass through a refining fire—a fire that will open up the unhealed wounds of the past so they can be lanced, purged, and cleansed, allowing them to be consumed by the healing power of God's love and, in this way, free up the gold within you. When Job came to a realization that facing and conquering his adversity would bless his life, he was able to do this. "When he hath tried me," Job said of God, "I shall come forth as gold" (Job 23:10).

I know this to be true. Others have realized it, and so can you. Becoming aware that I was a survivor of child sexual abuse brought me to a personal towering inferno. I felt like I was standing at the threshold of the inferno and could feel the heat from the intense fire penetrating to me from the other side of the door. When I touched the doorknob, I immediately jumped back in alarm. But I knew my task was to open the door and walk into the fierce flames—flames that would allow me to feel the feelings I had repressed as a child. I was very hesitant, afraid I would be consumed by the fire, by the pain of the feelings waiting inside the inferno. I was so afraid the fire had the power to consume me, I wondered if I could ever emerge intact.

However, I also believed that if I didn't enter the fire I would be stuck in a place I did not want to be. If I didn't go in, I would most likely regress and continue to spiral down into deeper feelings of shame, worthlessness, powerlessness, and self-defeat. Deep inside I knew the only way *out* was *through* the fire, by allowing myself to admit how worthless and powerless I really felt inside.

I finally decided to open the door and brave the fire. The pain and heat were so intense outside the inferno that I figured they couldn't be much worse inside. Once I was in the flames and dealing with the pain of the past, I wondered if I would survive, if I would ever live a life free of emotional trauma. Little by little, I learned what I needed to do to extinguish the fire and how to control the heat. In fact, I learned that some of the fire was actually good. I learned which parts of the fire to put out and which parts to harness to empower myself. At last, I felt I could walk through the fire to the door on the other side, then look back, knowing and feeling that I was made of pure gold—gold that gave me the power to not only survive but also to heal.

The purpose of this book is to aid you in your recovery once you have chosen to walk through the refining fire, the healing that will make you whole. I have not written this book to prove that sexual abuse and incest are real. I have not written it to declare statistical data and report research that supports the reality of the abuse of children. I have not written it to share graphic descriptions of how children are sexually abused and by whom. I have found that reading about descriptive accounts of another's sexual abuse can help some survivors, but it can also bury others in painful images that are counterproductive to healing.

This book offers you an uplifting and hopeful message: how to progress from being a victim of abuse to choosing to heal by coming unto Christ. Through clear explanations and practical suggestions, you will be led to focus on the recovery process while using the principles of the gospel of Jesus Christ as your foundation. As a Christian survivor, you will learn there are great powers of healing in your faith, prayers, and personal covenants.

This book is written in two parts. The first part, "The Path to Recovery" teaches you how to acknowledge and heal the past—to do the unfinished work of acknowledging and healing the wounds of your abuse. You will discover how to rescue and reclaim the little child who still hides inside you (whom I will refer to as your "Inner Child"). You will learn how to parent this "little person" so you can mature into the whole person you are meant to be. You will learn how to choose a therapist and a support group, and why talking about your abuse in a safe setting is profoundly healing. Included in each of these chapters are exercises I used and that other survivors have used to aid in the healing process. I know that the healing exercises I did weekly enhanced and accelerated my recovery.

In Part Two, "The Spiritual Path to Healing," you will learn how you can move forward spiritually. Until you learn how to manage and work through your spiritual anger, to grieve and heal your spiritual losses, you will not be able to integrate your spiritual self with all the other components of your healing. Your spiritual self is who you really are—the gold in you—and cannot be neglected during your healing process.

You will also learn about the process of forgiveness, and that coming to forgiveness takes time, and is a by-product of healing your emotional wounds. Some of the most important lessons covered in part two are taught in Chapter 9, "The Gift of the Atonement: A Healing Balm." Here you will learn how the powers of Christ's atonement can bring you to full and complete recovery. My hope is that you will learn these lessons well so they can effect a permanent change in your life.

In the Appendix you will find my husband's story of support. He shares the emotional and physical challenges my childhood abuse created in our relationship and how he came to deal with these challenges. The appendix also contains Recovery Resources, with information on books, newsletters, and organizations. The next section, called "Other's Paths," presents stories written by LDS survivors, using pseudonyms, that highlight particular aspects of the healing process. These stories represent a range of experiences that will probably reflect aspects of your own recovery. Although recovery is a complex and lengthy process that is not the same for any two individuals, reading other survivors' stories of recovery can be very therapeutic. The authors of these stories courageously share their experiences because each has a deep commitment to helping other survivors recover. Their stories are powerful testimonials of faith, hope, and determination. Each story bears witness that each survivor must travel at his or her own pace along the path to wholeness during the recovery experience.

Reading this book can help you become your own expert on how to manage your recovery. To heal you must become the judge of your own symptoms, determine what treatment to seek, and decide what kind of support you need. This book can provide tools and teach you principles that can lead to recovery, but it is up to you to apply the principles and use the tools—to put them into action.

Never underestimate your own resources: you have incredible power. Give as much commitment to healing in the present as you did to surviving in the past.

I believe all survivors have available to them a unique recovery resource—the gift of a higher powers which gives you special access to spiritual guidance in your recovery. Use this power to assist you in seeking help and making new decisions. Pray for the guidance of the Holy Ghost as you read this book and seek to understand the tools and principles taught herein.

As a survivor of sexual abuse, you have grown up wearing a mask. That mask hides the gold in you. You have been afraid to take it off, fearing what lies underneath, and what others might see. Your recovery will teach you how and when to take the mask off and how to let the refining fire burn off what you can't take off yourself. As you gain understanding of yourself, you will be appropriately wary of others' attempts to rip your mask off prematurely, leaving you with the pain and anguish of wounds you are not yet ready to uncover or not yet prepared to heal. The scriptures give the counsel not to "run faster than [you have] strength." (Mosiah 4:27), and this holds true for recovering from any kind of childhood trauma. Be careful not to turn over your decisions of what is right and wrong for you during your recovery to well-meaning friends, spouses, church leaders, or therapists. Use these individuals in appropriate ways—as advisors and support people. Trust only the Savior with your decisions, and you will experience in a profoundly personal way what it means to come unto him and be healed. And you will understand more fully how he is a partner in your healing and what your responsibility is.

Please believe that you cannot heal alone. It is extremely difficult, perhaps impossible, to heal from child sexual abuse in isolation. You should seek guidance and direction in finding the people you need to help you and support you throughout your entire recovery experience. Ideally you will combine many of the available resources in a way that is right for you.

At this point in your reading, you may wonder, "Is it worth it to go through recovery? It all sounds so hard." I can only share with you my feelings about the struggles and the rewards.

All through my recovery experience I often felt I had no one to turn to for help, no one to help relieve my emotional pain. All too often I felt extremely isolated and alone. I can remember sitting in church feeling as though I were the only one that had these trials. My feelings had become so tangible that it was as though I were wearing a garment of abuse that everyone could see but didn't want to recognize. I felt that I was a bad person because I had been abused, and I assumed everyone else had the same perception of me as I did. I can remember not wanting to go on living, feeling like my only choices were to live with this unbearable emotional pain or to take my life.

During these times I turned in desperation to my Heavenly Father, pleading for some relief. I have learned that relief *is* available to us through faith in our Savior, Jesus Christ, when we align our will with his. There is literal power in our faith; it is available to all of us, it is there to aid us in our trials. Not just the "I'm-having-a-bad-day" trials, but the gut-wrenching, soul-suffering, "I-can't-live-another-day" trials. I have learned that like most other principles of the gospel, receiving God's assistance is fairly simple. All we need to do is:

1. Know and believe the power is there.
2. Ask to have the power.
3. Receive it by trusting.

I have asked many times in my prayers for the power to heal the wounds of my past and for the knowledge of how to do so. At the times I felt a strong desire to end my life, I didn't act on those feelings because of the help I received as a direct answer to my prayers. In Matthew 7:7 we are taught: "Ask, and it shall be given you; seek, and ye shall find; knock, and it shall be opened unto you." (Also see 3 Nephi 14:7-8.) Christ has taught us throughout the scriptures that he will be there for us and help us to heal.

> But behold, he did deliver them because they did humble themselves before him; and because they cried mightily unto him he did deliver them out of bondage; and thus doth the Lord work with his power in all cases among the children of men, extending the arm of mercy towards them that put their trust in him. (Mosiah 29:20.)

> Feast upon the words of Christ; for behold, the words of Christ will tell you all things what ye should do. (2 Nephi 32:3.)

> I will go before your face. I will be on your right hand and on your left, and my Spirit shall be in your hearts, and mine angels round about you, to bear you up. (D&C 84:88.)

> But if ye will turn to the Lord with full purpose of heart, and put your trust in him, and serve him with all diligence of mind, if ye do this, he will, according to his own will and pleasure, deliver you out of bondage. (Mosiah 7:33.)

Patricia Pinegar, a member of the General Young Women Presidency of the Church of Jesus Christ of Latter-day Saints, teaches us a principle of healing in these words: "Even though we often feel inadequate, unworthy, or scared, if we will do all that we can, the Lord will do the rest to make us successful in what he has asked of us."[3]

I feel strongly that as a believer in Christ my recovery was accelerated through the aid of Christ's power. Elder Richard G. Scott has taught us that "recovery comes in steps. It is accelerated when gratitude is expressed to the Lord for every degree of improvement noted."[4]

I testify to you that I could not have done what I have had to do without God's help and Christ's power to assist me. As a result of choosing to recover from sexual abuse, I feel I have reclaimed my life. I now make choices and respond to life's experiences without the tragic events of the past influencing and controlling me. I now know what true inner joy and peace feel like—they come from within me and not from external conditions and experiences. I have experienced the gift of forgiveness by offering it to others who have hurt me. Having tasted of the fruit of the tree of life, which is the love of God, I feel that I have become a more pure vessel capable of offering my love and my service to all of God's children.

I know by experience that when we are looking for light and knowledge, we are going to get it, we are going to see it, we are going to feel it.

Make the choice to walk your path to wholeness. The time has never been more favorable for you to experience recovery. You have within your grasp tools to facilitate your healing and the gospel principles and powers to enhance your recovery experience. Choose to use them so that you may recover and be healed because "Jesus Christ maketh thee whole" (Acts 9:34). I pray that you will believe you have the God-given right to be whole.

1. Margery Williams, *The Velveteen Rabbit.* New York: Holt, Rinehart, and Winston, 1983, pp. 4-5.

2. Desktop Franklin Computer-Language Master Dictionary.

3. Patricia Pinegar, "New Young Women Presidency Called," *Ensign*, May 1992, p. 107.
4. Richard G. Scott, "Healing the Tragic Scars of Abuse," *Ensign*, May 1992, p. 32.

# CHAPTER 2
## REMEMBERING IS HEALING

*And ye shall know the truth, and the truth shall make you free. (John 8:32.)*

*...now it is high time to awake out of sleep: for now is our salvation nearer than when we believed.*
*The night is far spent, the day is at hand: let us therefore cast off the works of darkness, and let us put on the armour of light. (Romans 13:11, 12.)*

*M*emories of child sexual abuse are very painful. But remembering and recognizing them are crucial to recovery. Many survivors repress their abuse for years and then later, as adults, start to remember it. Others carry the memories deep within the cavities of their souls, convincing themselves that the abuse won't have an impact on their lives if they don't think about it or speak of it. And although they may not repress the memory of the abuse, they repress instead the feelings that have resulted from it. Other survivors may experience partial memories or memories that seem to come and go. Perhaps you can relate to one or more of these patterns.

Unresolved issues and unhealed wounds of child sexual abuse can have incredible power over the adult survivor. They can leave you crippled, chained with the pain of the past that prevents you from living the life you deserve. While trying to repress the shame that results, you also repress the joy of living and the love of self.

I did not start dealing with my experiences as an abused child until I reached a point I could no longer repress them. I finally had to deal with my memories and feelings in order to survive emotionally. Even though I was not experiencing abuse in my adult life, the scars of my past were so pervasive that they affected my sense of self, my sexuality, my intimate relationship with my husband, my parenting, my career, and most profoundly, my spiritual well-being.

I learned from my painful experiences that there is no strength in denial. I believe the adult survivor comes to a point where repression and denial can take far more emotional energy than doing the work of recovery. Once you start recovery work, you will find new reservoirs of energy and learn how you can use your memories and feelings to help you heal. You will find that they have incredible power to free you. I started this chapter with a scripture that says this well: "And ye shall know the truth, and the truth will make you free" (John 8:32). Christ has taught us that if we come unto him and use the power of the Holy Ghost, it will be given to us to "feel and see" (3 Nephi 18:25). You will find that you can ask Heavenly Father in prayer to help you feel and see all that is needful in order for you to become whole.

What you will feel and see will be different from any other survivor's experience. You must learn what is right for you in your recovery. Memories are a gift from God to aid you in your healing. I believe my memories were given to me as I needed them to heal throughout my recovery—to "feel and see" all I needed in order to heal and become whole. Since it was so difficult to know if what I was remembering was true, because it happened so long ago and was so painful to remember, I chose to ask for personal revelation concerning what really happened to me in my childhood.

I learned from the following scripture about the spirit of revelation within me that taught me what I needed to know throughout my recovery and continues to teach me:

> Behold, I say unto you they are made known unto me by the Holy Spirit of God. Behold, I have fasted and prayed many days that I might know these things of myself. And now I do know of myself that they are true; for the Lord God hath made them manifest unto me by his Holy Spirit; and this is the spirit of revelation which is in me. (Alma 5:46.)

## You Are Not Crazy—You Are Remembering

As your feelings and memories start to return, your first instinct may be to deny them. After all, that is what you have done your entire life in an effort to survive. You may feel like you are going crazy, and at times would rather believe you are crazy than accept the harsh reality of your abuse.

Perhaps you have grown up in an active religious family that presented the public image "All is well." You feared no one would believe what really happened, so you could hardly believe it yourself. "This cannot be," you tell yourself. "I tried so hard to do everything right. This couldn't have happened to me."

As I discovered the truth about myself, I realized that my compulsive need for perfection and over-achievement came from my tremendous feelings of worthlessness. Because my core self was so damaged, I created an overachieving self upon which I depended for self-worth. An obsessive desire for perfection as an adult—trying to do everything "just right"—may be the result of *your* abuse, of your need to make up for your feelings of shame and worthlessness.

As the shame inside rises to the surface, you may feel that you wear it like a dirty garment that others can see and are repulsed by. You may find that going to church and socializing with others is very painful and uncomfortable. You may only feel safe when you are alone and undisturbed.

The authors of *Recovery: A Guide for Adult Children of Alcoholics* offer this advice to adult survivors:

> There is an old proverb that goes like this: "The truth will make you free, but first it will make you miserable." But, yes, it really is necessary, and it really is safe, to dethrone the tyranny of your past. No pain is so devastating as the pain a person refuses to face, and no suffering so lasting as the suffering left unacknowledged. Hidden pain becomes a tyrant determining where you can go, what you can do, and when you are comfortable. As a child, you may have found it necessary to bury certain traumatizing experiences. If a child is being abused emotionally, physically, or sexually, and believes there is no one to turn to for help, the child might think, "It's not really that bad. It's no big deal. In fact, it doesn't even bother me that much." Such denial can allow children to live through horrors that, if fully comprehended at the time, could be devastating. To bury the pain as a child is to ensure survival as a child. [1]

The "crazy stage," when you feel you may be losing your sanity, is the beginning of recognizing and dealing with your reality. Please keep in mind that it is only a stage and that your feelings of craziness, shame, and guilt will subside as you learn why you have repressed and dissociated yourself from your abuse, why your memories are beginning to return to you, and what types of memories you may be experiencing.

## Dissociation and Repression

As a child your only means of surviving the trauma of your abuse may have been to create an experience that denied reality. Like me, you may have pretended to be asleep, thought about being somewhere else, or concentrated on an object or an image in your room so much that you felt a part of it. In order to survive your trauma you needed to detach, or dissociate yourself, from the trauma.

I have interviewed several survivors who have experienced Multiple Personality Disorder, and I have read extensively about it. As professionals continue to learn more about MPD, they are discovering that children who repeatedly experience horrific episodes of sexual and ritual abuse create other selves, other personalities as a way to survive the trauma. These personalities contain their shame, guilt, fear, powerlessness, anger, and rage. Often the survivor develops a personality for each feeling. Survivors who experience multiple personalities are not able to construct a unified reality because parts of their reality are too traumatic to be integrated. So they create others to take charge, leaving the abused self abandoned and lost.

I created a false self because my core self, my real self was ashamed. I covered it up because it was too painful to exist in the core, real self. I hid my shame, I became superhuman, needing to do everything perfectly. I did not know how to be human; I could not be who I was because my real self was too full of pain.

I have discovered that some children even create an out-of-body experience in order to escape the pain and trauma of their abuse. If this is true of your experience, please know that you did it so you would not have to stay mentally present to experience the shame and pain of your abuse. One survivor states:

> *At age nine, I can remember floating in the corner of the room as I witnessed my body being raped by my friend's fifteen-year-old brother. I was spending the night at her home. I couldn't stand to live through the trauma again. I had been a victim several other times in my life and never knew how to stop it. I chose to leave my body in order to survive.*
>
> *—A Survivor*

When your trauma was over, you may have chosen to forget about the experience, to dissociate yourself from it, repressing your reality little by little. Or you may have created a vague, dreamlike place in your mind for what you experienced, in order to create the illusion that it didn't really happen. Just as our bodies have the power to go into physical shock in order to block physical pain, our conscious minds have the power to block and repress horrible traumatizing experiences. I found that dissociating and repressing my childhood pain and trauma was a God-given mechanism that protected me until I became strong enough and mature enough, emotionally and physically, to do the work necessary to heal.

After interviewing many incest survivors I realized that this is especially true in surviving incest. If you are an incest survivor, you were probably forced to live with your perpetrator. Alice Miller, well-known Inner Child psychoanalyst and author, teaches us that living in an incestuous family can be more traumatic than living as a prisoner in a prisoner-of-war camp. A prisoner of war has a very clear picture of the enemy. Even after experiencing abuse at the hands of the enemy, the survivor is returned to the support of other fellow prisoners.

*As a child living with incest, I did not have a clear picture of who my enemy was. I think there were several reasons for this. The person inflicting shame and pain on me was also the person I was being taught to trust and love. I was being taught at church that I was in a "forever family" with "parents kind and dear." I knew I was dependent on my family for physical survival. I tried to tell someone of my trauma only to be treated with shock and disapproval. I heard: "Your parents are such good people, how could you say something like that about them?" My reaction as a child was one of guilt and confusion and finally belief that the person saying this must be right. I said to myself: "I must be bad and crazy."*

*The only way I could make sense out this mass of confusion in my childlike mind was to block and repress my abuse and create a "fantasy family." I grew up believing in my fantasy family, making choices that reinforced its reality in my life. My fantasy was stitched together with the belief that I had a great childhood, with great parents. But these stitches began fraying when I reached adulthood, exposing my harsh reality more and more: I did not have a great childhood. I had very wounded parents who did not care for me properly.*

*By choosing to recover, I trusted my inner self enough to be willing to undo the stitches of denial that have held my false self together for so long. I yearn to heal; I yearn to offer myself and my posterity a better life.*

*—A Survivor*

## Post Traumatic Stress Disorder

Post Traumatic Stress Disorder (PTSD) is a clinical

diagnosis given to soldiers who continue to mentally relive many of their most traumatic war experiences, as well as to individuals who have been traumatized by natural disasters or who have witnessed violent crimes. PTSD is often the official diagnosis for the survivor of incest and child sexual abuse.

PTSD is the delayed release of these feelings and memories. It is as though they have been frozen and are beginning to thaw. The unresolved feelings and forgotten memories are triggered by familiar smells, sounds, experiences, or even events that mimic the original trauma.

I experienced PTSD in my early thirties. I have since discovered that memories and feelings commonly start surfacing in an adult survivor's life between ages thirty and forty-five. Some major life events triggered my feelings before I had any memories. I was experiencing feelings of powerlessness, helplessness, hopelessness, fear, terror, great anger, and rage. I was a time-bomb of buried memories without consciously knowing it.

I was experiencing severe depression, mood swings that were uncontrollable; what I would get angry about did not justify the amount of powerful emotion that was released.

I was feeling very much isolated and alone, as though there were no other LDS women on the face of the earth with similar feelings. I expressed tremendous confusion and despair. I wondered where this was coming from, and why I had so much emotional trauma in my life when I was trying to live the gospel. There was nothing in my adult life to explain what I was going through.

Even if you have lived with no conscious memory of your abuse, your body retains the feelings of what happened to you. Your body stores unresolved trauma in your tissues, and your brain has the power to repress painful events stored in your subconscious mind. "When anyone is violated, the first feeling response is raw fear and terror.

One wants to run away from the threat and fear. One is helpless and out of control. The more the situation is intolerable, the greater the need is to dissociate. The body records and imprints the terror. Later the feelings of hurt, anger, abandonment and shame are recorded."[2]

> *When I had memories return, people asked me, "If you forgot so much of this for so long.... why dig it up now?" They need to understand that we did not "dig" it up; it just comes up suddenly and unexpectedly. Sometimes it is disguised as severe depression, physical problems, dreams, or as just plain memories which can flood us for no apparent reason. It can be very scary and upsetting.*
>
> *—A Survivor [3]*

## Types of Memories

Memories return in many ways. Flashbacks, dreams, body memories involving senses, and regression memories are some of the most common.

### Flashbacks

Flashbacks are memories without distance. They come into your mind suddenly and without reason. They are like watching a movie of yourself or of someone else. They may be accompanied by the feelings you felt at the time of your abuse—feelings like fear, shame, and powerlessness. These feelings may come up suddenly and may cause you to panic. Flashbacks bring with them all the terror of the original event. They can be almost continuous and overwhelming. They are often triggered by something very ordinary, like someone walking up to you from behind, conversations, words, or movies. Smells, touch, and sounds may also trigger flashbacks.

Survivors often feel like they are going crazy because these flashbacks are often uncontrollable and occur in no specific order. They are like pieces of a jigsaw puzzle that don't seem to make sense. But with time and healing, they do fit. Keep in mind that confusion is often the beginning of healing and that it is possible to move forward with the confusion. Another reason survivors who experience flashbacks feel like they are going crazy is because the false memories they have created of their childhood conflict with the truth that surfaces through their conscious minds.

Become familiar with what triggers each flash of memory. Try to identify the events and conditions of the present that seem to give rise to each flashback. This may be difficult since you may have delayed reactions. The triggering event may have happened a day or two before. Acknowledge the flashback for what it is—a window to your past. Keep in mind that you are an adult now with the power to protect yourself from your memory—to care for yourself. If the flashback occurs when you feel you cannot deal with it, make a note of it and plan a time to work through it, including the feelings associated with it. Be sure to do this work in a safe environment, when you don't feel pressured and you won't be interrupted by others.

When I experienced flashbacks, I became a child again. I felt as though I were in a small body, reliving the particular events with all the feeling, words, sounds, and people that originally caused my grief. I saw the person who had inflicted the pain on me. This triggered the uncontrollable feelings I was never allowed to have as a child.

## Dream Memories

Several of the survivors I interviewed experienced what I call *dream memories*. Dreams can allow the repressed realities of our past to leak out. Conscious thought can be controlled and altered by defenses, but in our dreams our minds seem to have no boundaries. Many survivors have dreams about being powerless with feelings of entrapment and fear as a common theme—dreams about falling in mid-air, being chased, needing to respond to a given situation or person and having no power to act. The same held true for dreams that were horror-filled and terrifying, full of images of entrapment and violence. Survivors felt these dreams were symbolic of their childhood abuse.

You may dream of aspects of your actual abuse but the identity of the perpetrator may be masked. As you experience dream memory, start keeping a dream journal to aid you in your recovery. Keep a notebook next to your bed and use it to jot down any memory you have of a dream as soon as you awaken, before you get out of bed. This will allow you the most clarity in remembering details. Share your dreams with your therapist or in a support group and learn what is most beneficial to you. Learn to use this powerful tool for remembering.

> *As I slept my dreams seemed profoundly real and frightening. When I woke I realized they were not real; that they were teaching me about how I really felt inside. I allowed myself to be taught by them. When I experienced a dream memory, I would stay in the same position I had been sleeping in while I recalled and recorded the dream. If I had to get out of bed to get writing materials, I would return to my same position, which allowed me more recall.*
>
> —*A Survivor*

## Body and Sense Memory

For many survivors the most powerful medium of memory comes to them through the body, not the mind. Our bodies don't forget the trauma of the past. Our sense of smell, touch, sight, taste, and hearing, cue us into experiences that stimulated a particular sense in the past. The feeling of something wet on your skin, the smell of sweat, being in a totally dark room, the sound of footsteps behind you—all of these can feel overwhelmingly threatening and dangerous. My body memories were very potent. If anyone approached me from behind unknowingly I became frantic. It was very difficult for me to engage in sexual relations with my husband during the first stages of recovery. I felt as if I were a child being abused once again. I needed to know I didn't have to have sex when it felt so frightening. I needed to know I could say "no," something I didn't know how to say as a child. When I shared with my husband these feelings of my need to abstain from sexual relations, he agreed for as long as I needed to, and several months went by, but not without pain and confusion in respect to this part of our relationship. I'm grateful he supported me to take the time I needed to work through this and to maintain my right to say "no."

You may experience both body and cognitive memory. However, I have found that some survivors only experience body memory. One survivor asked, "Does it matter if I can't quite remember specific details of what happened when I was little? Can I still heal?"

My answer is this: If you don't have a cognitive, visual memory of what happened to you but a sensory memory instead, this feeling may be telling you that you were indeed abused in some way, and very likely the abuse was to your body. If you are a survivor in this predicament, please believe this: You know what you know.

Yes, you can heal without cognitive, visual memories. I have known survivors who never did have specific cognitive, visual memories to work with in recovery, but who successfully worked with what they did have, and were able to begin the healing process.

*I don't know who you are. I don't know where you are. I don't have exact pictures of what you did to me, but I do know you molested me. The pictures may not be there, but that doesn't change the reality of my feelings.*

*— A Survivor[4]*

## Regression

In the early stages of my recovery I attended a John Bradshaw workshop where I learned about original pain work or what I call *age-regression visualization work*. Age-regression visualization work is going back to your childhood memory and trying to recall painful events. You can do this by allowing yourself to regress in age as you visualize places and events, then by allowing your memories to resurface.

Through age-regression visualization work, I found it possible to return to my childhood and retrieve memories. A trained therapist can help you do this. A competent therapist is also one who will assist you in discovering your truth, not one who will try to tell you what your truth is. You can come to a realization of your abuse through memories or feelings, have it confirmed by God, and then have it affirmed by those who can help you overcome its effects in your life. I, myself, never had a therapist suggest to me that I might have been sexually abused as a child. In fact, I didn't even begin therapy until my first memories returned.

Be very careful of therapists who try to tell you what you think and remember—those who feel a need to diagnose you. A good therapist will guide you in the path of self-discovery and healing, reinforcing your belief that you can lead the way. Some therapists may try to convince you to retrieve all memories of your abusive experiences in vivid detail. I don't believe that is necessary. I believe we remember as much as we need to remember in order to heal.

While some discovery is vital to the healing process, the unnecessary probing by others into unrevealed past memories can be traumatic in a way that is not good for us.

Retrieve your memories as necessary. You are the one who manages your recovery. Remember that unrevealed memories are not the same as denial of memories. As a result of prayer and fasting, you will know what you need to remember by being enlightened by the spirit of truth. "Behold, thou knowest that thou hast inquired of me and I did enlighten thy mind; and now I tell thee these things that thou mayest know that thou hast been enlightened by the Spirit of truth" (Doctrine and Covenants 6:15). "For the Spirit speaketh the truth and lieth not. Wherefore, it speaketh of things as they really are, and of things as they really will be; wherefore, these things are manifested unto us plainly, for the salvation of our souls" (Jacob 4:13).

Keep in mind there are other ways of recalling your memories that I have not included in this book and there are as many unique experiences as there are survivors. I have described only some of the most common. For books that offer more information on remembering, please refer to Recovery Resources in the Appendix.

My own experience and the experience of other survivors is that many of us who have been abused repress our painful experiences in increments, and our memory of them tends to return in increments. When memories start to return, you may not always know what they mean right away. You need to allow yourself time to work with each memory, moving at a pace you are comfortable with. The pace I found comfortable was to work with my memories daily for several days, then to take a break and make a conscious effort to focus on the present. By doing this I learned to pace myself and my healing process so that I wouldn't become overwhelmed. Pacing yourself will help you better manage your recovery. Kelly R. Fielding, a professional therapist, says this:

> A recent review of the literature on treatment of adults molested as children suggests that there is an important "window of opportunity" that must be maintained for survivors experiencing distressing memories. There are two factors that need to be carefully balanced in order for this "window" to remain open and accessible. First, the individual must be willing to exert a consistent amount of stress on him or herself for the purpose of slowly resurrecting the memories and accompanying emotion. Second, the memories and emotions cannot be so intense that they become overwhelming, thereby causing the individual to shut down the healing process out of the natural defense to avoid pain.[5]

When you decide to share your memories with a therapist, church leader, or friend, make sure your listener is safe and supportive. Remember—you are starting to recall an experience that requires a commitment to truths few may want to hear, to things few want to say, to memories nobody wants to have.

If you share your memories inappropriately with individuals who don't have the experience or capacity to validate you, this can cause you to once again repress your memories, strengthening your self-denial. The child in you, your Inner Child, needs to be believed and supported, not abandoned, threatened and violated again. Allow yourself to affirm your memories by carefully choosing who you share them with.

Early in the process of remembering, you will probably feel as though you are going to remember more then you can handle. Later you may come to a point in your healing where you will feel as though you can't remember enough and you will want more, and then you will have to learn to let go so that God may lead you.

> *At the beginning of my recovery all I knew was that I had been molested as a child. I had memories return of non-family perpetrators but I also felt strongly I could be a survivor of incest. So I went to my Heavenly Father in prayer and asked him if I was a survivor of incest. I was committed to do the work of my recovery and felt I was ready to deal with this trauma if it were true.*
>
> *The answer I was given came to me very clearly: "You are doing what you need to be doing now in your recovery, continue to heal the memories you do have. It is not necessary for you to know the answer right now." I did not receive a yes or a no answer, just a "not now." I came to learn several months later the answer and could then see why I didn't need to know the first time I asked. I could see that I had not been in a safe place in my life to deal with this reality.*
>
> *—A Survivor*

You have probably been displacing your powerful and painful emotions onto experiences in your adult life that do not justify the emotion you are giving them. In the first stages of recovery the events of remembering and the experience of feeling the feelings associated with my abuse often occurred erratically and randomly. As a survivor I decided my task was to bring the two together. As John Bradshaw taught at his workshop, "You have come to a point in your life where the raging dog in the basement needs to be let out before it escapes on its own, hurting you and many others in the process." You are starting to get your memories;

now you can connect the memories with the painful feelings of your childhood.

It is time for you, as it was once for me, to "awake from a deep sleep, yea, even from the sleep of hell, and shake off the awful chains by which ye are bound, which are the chains which bind the children of men [and women], that they are carried away captive down to the eternal gulf of misery and woe" (2 Nephi 1:13). I found that remembering was healing because my personal knowledge was my truth, and my truth gave me freedom.

## A Personal Essay

The following essay contains profound insights into the healing experience of remembering the deeply painful experience of child sexual abuse. It was written by a survivor who was sexually abused for eight years by her father, from age eight to age sixteen. The first incident took place the day after she was baptized.

## The Closet

Once there was a young girl who was very sad and alone. She had many heartaches that she had to carry all by herself. When they became too difficult for her to bear, she would box them up and stuff them on a shelf in her closet. She felt it was the only way she could insure her survival. As the years went by, the closet became so full of bad feelings and memories that they even dirtied the happy and pleasant memories.

One day when she went to stuff more things in the closet, she opened the door and everything came tumbling down on top of her. No matter how hard she tried, she couldn't put it all back. She needed help, but it wasn't a pleasant job. The people she reached out to either ran away or scolded her for saving it all in the first place. They didn't understand. She was just about to give up when she decided to ask for help just once more. She prayed that she would be able to find a person who would be willing and able to help her. Someone who would understand. Someone who would really care. And her prayer was answered.

At first she was afraid to share with this new person. Would this new person ridicule or condemn her? Would she understand about the pain and the heartache? As time went on, the girl learned to trust her new friend. With love and respect, the friend would open up the boxes and together they would examine the contents. When the pleasant memories were opened, the friend would blow off the dust and say, "This is a happy memory. Let's save this one." And they would put it neatly on the shelf. When they came to the ugly dirty boxes, the friend would help her search for and salvage anything of possible value, put it in a clean box, and throw the old box away.

Sometimes the friend would pick up boxes the girl didn't like. The girl would tell her, "Just throw those out. They have bad feelings in them." But the friend would open them anyway. After examining the contents, she would say, "These aren't bad feelings. They serve a very important purpose. Let's clean them, put them in a new box, and save them for a while. Maybe you will feel differently about them later." So they put them on the bottom shelf to re-evaluate later.

They continued to sort, clean, and organize. Sometimes the girl would become so sad and tired she wanted to give up. She felt overwhelmed by the hard work. At these times, her patient and understanding friend would take her by the hand and give her love and strength.

One day the girl looked around and discovered there was just a very small pile left. The closet was neat and orderly. And there was plenty of room to store happy memories for many years to come. The girl also realized that she felt better than she had for many years. She reached out, took her friend by the hand and said, "My dearest friend, you have stood by my side when no one else could, or would. At times, your kindness and genuine concern have been my life line. I have felt peace and sisterhood in your presence and love in your touch. Those gifts I will always treasure.[6]

## Exercises that Help You Heal

I found the following exercises most helpful as memories return:

1. Relax. What you are dealing with is only a memory. You are safe now and no one can harm you. If you run from the memory and allow yourself to be shackled by the feelings of fear and powerlessness accompanied by the memory, you become the abused child again, as if you were five years old again and the abuse is happening now. But it is not happening now. You are an adult with the power and ability to take care of yourself.

2. If you have small children, call someone to watch them for several hours (allowing you to leave) or if you prefer to stay in your home, take the children somewhere else to be tended. You need to realize you are in no condition at the moment to be a healthy functioning parent, and you will be doing the best thing for them by separating yourself from them. Find a safe place where you can feel comfortable and unthreatened. If you need to be with someone you can depend on and trust, call them and ask them to come by or arrange to visit them.

3. It can be very helpful to write about what you are remembering and how it makes you feel in a recovery journal. Express yourself honestly. Nobody is going to read it if you keep it in a safe place.

4. Take time to recover. Memories can be very emotionally and physically exhausting and draining. You will feel vulnerable and nervous, so take time to comfort and nurture yourself. Take time to be alone, to exercise, to take a walk, or to share your memories and feelings with someone safe. Talking will help reinforce your belief that this unpleasant memory is something in your past and nothing that is happening to you now.

5. Remember that your Inner Child, your real self, is telling you about her life and pain. She wants to know if it's safe to disclose her secret and if you can be trusted. The wounded Inner Child is very aware that your adult self is still a victim. She has to learn how to take care of you and herself. By taking care of yourself in the present, you will prove to your Inner Child that you are an adult worthy and capable of taking care of her, thereby earning her trust. This will accelerate your healing experience and strengthen your ability to work with future memories.

1. Herbert L. Gravitz and Julie D. Bowen, *Recovery: A Guide for Adult Children of Alcoholics*, New York: Simon & Schuster, 1985, p. 37.
2. John Bradshaw, *Bradshaw on the Family* (Deerfield Beach, Florida: Health Communications, Inc., 1988), p. 115.
3. *In Reflection*, monthly newsletter, (Portland, Oregon: June 1992), Vol. 2, No. 3, p. 7.
4. *In Reflection*, monthly newsletter, (Portland, Oregon: June 1992), Vol. 2, No. 3, p. 5.
5. Kelly R. Fielding, Ph.D., *In Reflection*, monthly newsletter, (Portland, Oregon: June 1992), Vol. 2, No. 3, p. 4.
6. Name Withheld, *Exponent II* (1987), Vol. 14, No. 1.

# CHAPTER 3
## FEELING IS HEALING

*As a child, I learned that strength was the denial of feeling. Now I see that feeling is the key to self-honesty. Within feeling is found the passion for change.*[1]

*E*ach of us functions through a combination of our intellect, will, and feelings. The delicate balance of all three is crucial to our well-being. Feelings and emotions are given to us from God; they are unique parts in his plan of creation. They enable us to receive the kind of inspiration from him that will guide us through this mortal experience. If we distort, deny, or repress any of our feelings, we are out of harmony with ourselves because feelings are the medium through which the Holy Ghost communicates to us. Parley P. Pratt teaches us how the Holy Ghost can enhance our capacity to feel and grow spiritually:

> The Holy Ghost's influence quickens all the intellectual faculties, increases, enlarges, expands and purifies all the natural affections and passions and adopts them by the gift of wisdom to their lawful use. It inspires, develops, cultivates, and matures all the fine tuned sympathies, joys, tastes, kindred feeling and affections of our nature.[2]

Remembering your traumatic childhood—and allowing yourself to feel the trauma—enables you to experience and manage the feelings you repressed as a child. Learning about the feelings you could not feel as a child will help you accept and work through them. The more accepting you are of your feelings, the safer you will feel as you allow more memories and feelings to resurface and to teach you.

I found that I had to learn to accept my feelings whenever they surfaced; I couldn't choose when they would come. At times I feared that the floodgate I had been using to dam up my emotions would open so far that feelings would flood my life and leave me overwhelmed. Please know that as your feelings begin to surface, you will learn to ride the waves by managing them appropriately.

## Feelings Are Like Colors

As a child I was taught not to have feelings like anger, sadness, hopelessness, and worthlessness. I was told they were bad feelings, and so I was not allowed to express them. When I did express them, many of the adults in my life tried to convince me that I was wrong. "You really don't feel that way," I was told. "Stop thinking about it and you will feel better. Think a happy thought and the bad thoughts will go away."

I decided that I would control my feelings in my head, by thinking positive thoughts. I believed that this would make everything okay. But I only succeeded in suppressing the feelings. I realized that I spent so much time trying to "figure it out" that I didn't allow myself to "feel it out." The false beliefs I was taught as a child left me believing I was bad if I had "bad emotions," often called "negative emotions."

Another survivor shares her insights:

> *Mankind has devalued feelings. Feelings are "worthless"; feelings must be controlled, put away,*

*denied, covered up. We must not feel them if they are bad; we should only feel good feelings. Painful, suffering feelings are to be hidden, ignored; they are stupid; they cause weakness.*

*We have been taught that the intellect is of great value; it is of great worth—show it off, take care of it, teach it, nurture it, fill it up, be proud of it, use it to control your feelings.*

*— A Survivor*

I often hear adults apologize for how they are feeling—for expressing their feelings with tears. "I'm so sorry I'm crying," they say. "I don't know why I'm crying. I wish I were stronger. I don't know what's the matter with me."

A common false belief is that denial of feeling builds inner strength. The truth is that self-honesty and the appropriate expression of feelings takes strength and courage and builds more strength.

At this point, I'd like to suggest that the negative or "bad" emotions we've been discussing are actually *healing* emotions. This is because your feelings are a pure part of your being. Emotion alone does not define who you are, especially if you cling to false beliefs. Shame, worthlessness, and powerlessness are only feelings. They are not who you are. Allowing yourself to experience all your feelings will enable you to find out who you really are and will generate feelings of love, joy, peace, happiness, enthusiasm, and other pleasurable emotions.

A good friend of mine taught me that feelings are like colors. Just as there are no bad or wrong colors, there are no bad or wrong feelings. Just as there is a rainbow of colors, there is a rainbow of feelings we experience in this life. Healing comes when we allow ourselves and our Inner Child to feel and acknowledge the rainbow of feelings within us.

## Fear of Feeling

The event of remembering and the experience of feeling long-buried emotion doesn't come when we choose; it comes when it comes. It tends to be erratic, occurring randomly during the first stages of recovery. As a survivor you have the task to integrate the emotion you buried as a child with the memory you have of your childhood abuse.

It was very frightening and threatening to me as an adult to feel the shame, worthlessness, and powerlessness I had felt as a child, and I wondered if I would have to continue to live in a constant state of fear. As my feelings surfaced, I learned to tell myself that these were temporary, but healing, emotions.

As an abused child my first reaction to what was happening to me was fear and panic, most likely because I was told to keep quiet; perhaps I was even threatened with my life. Those feelings of fear and panic were unavoidable; I had to face them. You were probably told to keep quiet about your abuse, too, and that you or someone else close to you would be hurt if you ever told. Most abused children are scared into silence.

As feelings and memories return, you may feel that you are that child again, experiencing all the fear you felt when you were abused. As an adult, you may even find that telling another person about your abuse now is still threatening, because the child in you still fears that the abuser's threats will come to pass.

In reality, your Inner Child does not have to fear the threats anymore because you are now an adult in an adult's body. And you have chosen to heal your Inner Child by allowing yourself to feel how scared, how bad, how powerless you really felt all those years ago.

If your fear is extremely intense, it may block the other emotions linked to your abuse. This does not mean the feelings are not there. It means you are not ready to feel them yet. Please know that it is okay to remember and not to feel. Your feelings will come as you learn to handle them.

When I started remembering my abuse, I didn't want to believe it. I pretended it was a bad dream or scenes from a bad movie I'd seen and that it never really happened to me. I was afraid of the filth, the ugliness that was created by this horrible tragedy. When I first visualized my abuse, I could see it, but not feel it. I was completely numb, internally and externally numb.

I was with a supportive friend. She said it was okay to see it and not feel it—the feelings would come when I was ready. She helped so much. The pictures were clear; the information was there and it explained so many things in my life that I never had answers to.

When you start to re-experience your childhood feelings of fear, shame, and powerlessness, your first response will probably be to deny them and repress them. If this is the case, it may be because you still want to believe the fantasy of denial that your false self has created.

I remember waking up one night, my memory and feelings trying to work their way out. I kept trying to swallow them, push them back down again and again. I finally let the feelings come, the events roll forward. I started rocking at my hips, crying and crying. I felt anger, confusion, and again the denial of my abuse—pretending that I was making it up, that it couldn't happen to such a nice little girl.

I decided to go to my Inner Child and I visualized a heavenly mother that would come with me, to hold her and rock her. I felt heavenly mother was with her and I was finally able to go back to sleep.

Still, the next day I thought this must all be in my head because I had done such a good job of pushing it out of my mind all of my life.

You may be afraid of your feelings because you think

that once you start feeling them you may not survive them. Perhaps you believe your pain has the power to destroy you. When you have repressed your feelings for a long time, it is natural to be wary of what might happen once they are released. But the existence of powerful feelings does not mean that they will destroy you, that you won't be able to manage them.

By not actively and safely expressing your feelings, you run the risk of having them explode unpredictably in situations that may not merit such powerful emotional reactions. You are doing yourself and others a favor by choosing to work through your feelings privately, with a therapist or in a support group, rather then letting them leak out randomly. Remember, you will not be imprisoned or destroyed by your feelings. Though they may make you temporarily uncomfortable, you are on the path to freedom.

At times during my recovery I felt overwhelmed by the powerful emotions that surfaced. It was as though I were raw flesh moving through the day. At other times I felt completely numb, like a zombie moving through endless space. During these times I had to keep telling myself, "It is okay to feel just the way you feel. You don't have to fix it or get rid of it. Allow yourself to feel it and release it."

>  *It's as though your body is being taken over and there is nothing you can do about it.*
>
> — *A Survivor*

> *I knew in my head what I was supposed to do and what I needed to do, but my feelings made me want to run away and leave my pain behind.*
>
> —*A Survivor*

> *When I ran from feelings that were starting to*

*come up, I allowed them to build up and become more potent until they burst out and spilled all over me and everybody around me.*

*—A Survivor*

There may be times when you will feel so bad you will want to die. At times during the most difficult part of my recovery, my feelings were so overwhelming that I felt like my body was filled with something rotten and that if I could make an opening in my skin, somehow the pressure would be relieved and the rottenness would spill out and I could feel some relief. I know feelings of despair and self-hate are authentic; they should not be denied.

At the same time, it is essential that you do not act on these feelings. It is never okay to hurt yourself. As real as these feelings of self-loathing may seem, they are generated by false beliefs and lies. You deserve to live and be happy. Every time you fight back by not acting on fear and self-hate, you fight against the brainwashing of your abuser, and this time you win. Continue to fight back by not hurting yourself, by not acting on your impulse to destroy yourself. You are a champion because you have already survived the worst. You deserve to live, to love, and to be loved.

## Anger: Moving Through and Past It

In Chapter 2, I refer to one of the first stages of recovery as the "crazy stage"—the stage where memories and feelings start to surface, when fear and panic descend. My experience led me to believe that the crazy stage usually evolves to the anger stage.

Learning the significance of my anger and rage was a very important part of my healing experience. I realized anger was a powerful emotion that could help me to heal if it was expressed appropriately. In *The Courage to Heal*, I read that "anger does not have to be an uncontrolled, uncontrollable phenomenon. As you welcome your anger and become familiar with it, you can direct it to meet your needs—like an experienced rider controlling a powerful horse."[3]

For instance, in the beginning of my recovery, when I did not manage and direct my anger appropriately, it would be triggered by events like children arguing, or family members leaving messes. My unchanneled anger would hurt my family and leave me guilt-ridden.

Anger is probably one of the least understood and most socially unacceptable emotions. All too often, it is placed in the "bad" emotion category. Because of this, many survivors of child sexual abuse refuse to acknowledge their anger or they may feel guilty for being angry. Refusing to acknowledge your anger does not make it go away. Unexpressed anger stays inside of you and inhibits your healing process, reinforcing all the false beliefs you are trying to dispel. Unexpressed anger tends to fuel self-destructive thoughts like "I am bad, I am worthless, I deserve to die, I am wrong, I am to blame."

If you begin to feel angry emotions, please do not feel guilty. Your anger is a natural response to your abuse. It is okay to be angry about being abused—especially about being sexually abused. You and your Inner Child are worth being angry for. Getting angry at the abuser helps you remember and feel your innocence. You are justified in being angry about what happened to you as a child.

Just as Jesus expressed his anger toward the money changers in the temple because they were defiling a holy place, you have the right to express your anger about another person defiling your body, which is also a holy temple. Anger itself is not sin. We sin only if we use the anger to generate destructive or harmful actions. In the New Testament, Paul teaches us this: "Be ye angry, and sin not" (Ephesians 4:26).

The only risks involved in feeling the deep roots of your anger are expressing it destructively and getting stuck in it. Anger can make you feel a false sense of power, especially when you've come from a position of powerlessness. We need to be careful not to misdirect anger at society, at the church, or at innocent people. When we feel angry at everyone who is the abuser's gender or resentment at social and religious systems that we feel have failed us, these emotions are too amorphous to be helpful.

Anger can feel so good, so empowering, that it can be mistaken for recovery, but it is only one of the first steps toward recovery. Like all survivors, you need to experience your anger so you can move through it into healing and recovery. From anger springs the energy that can move you out of victimization into life.

It was easy for me to be angry about my church experience. I was mad that I had experienced a type of adversity I couldn't talk freely about. I saw other church members who were offered compassionate service when they were struggling with health or financial problems. It made me mad that I was not offered the same support. Because I felt so justified in my anger, it was not easy to move past it. I had to realize that my anger could not change other people, that it was only hurting me and my family—not the people I was actually angry with. In time, I learned to release my anger by using appropriate exercises that helped me begin to heal.

If we do not put boundaries on our anger, it can destroy ourselves and others. Recognize what your anger is about and who you are really angry at. Are you really mad at your husband just for being a man? Does your three-year-old really deserve all that rage because he marked on the wall with a magic marker? Or are your feelings actually tapping into repressed anger from your childhood? Are you displacing your anger onto people and events that do not deserve it? Aren't you really mad at your abuser and what he or she did to you? Give yourself permission to express that anger in ways that will allow you more and more freedom and keep you from displacing your anger inappropriately.

*I got so tired of losing control and allowing myself to be angry at people and situations that didn't deserve my rage.*

*I had to learn to be angry with the people and situations I was really enraged with. I was enraged at my father for molesting me. I was enraged at my mother for allowing it to happen. I was really ticked off that I had lived so many years with all this pain stuck inside of me. I was angry at feeling cheated out of a childhood. I was fighting mad about a lot of things in my past, but was dumping it on everyone in my present.*

*I didn't phone my parents and start screaming at them, but I chose to set boundaries with them that helped me feel safe. I asked my parents not to contact me for a while, because I needed time alone. If they did not honor my boundaries I learned to tell them how it made me feel and expressed my anger with assertiveness and clarity.*

*It was also helpful to work through my anger by writing letters to my parents and family about what I was angry about. I only felt safe to mail a few of these letters. I did anger meditations where I would allow my little child to express her anger to her parents. When I felt as though I had to do something physical with my anger, I would exercise, or go into my room and punch pillows, pretending the pillow was the person I was angry at. I figured that if punching pillows helped me feel better, it was a better choice then hurting someone.*

—*A Survivor*

Rage was a powerful emotion that seemed to come from nowhere and fill my whole body. I had to learn to recognize what triggered this deep-seated emotion and learn to diffuse it. One of the most painful experiences I had with rage was an afternoon I found my toddler son drawing on a wall with magic markers. I went crazy. I knew enough not to hurt him, but I felt like I could. I took myself into the other room and broke a chair, screaming and agonizing at the same time. My children fled from me. An unpredictable raging mother of four small children is not a pretty sight, but it was my reality. I called my husband at work, pleading for him to come home. He came home immediately because he knew I was not safe alone with the children. We were all scared and I was feeling very, very guilty as I sat and wept. Jon insisted I call my counselor, which I did, and she was able to see me that day.

In her office she told me that I needed immediate help. Here I was, a mother at home alone from fourteen to sixteen hours a day with an infant, a two-, a three-, and a six-year-old. At the same time, I was a woman recovering from traumatic child sexual abuse. I could not "escape" my house to go anywhere alone; my children were totally dependent on me. My therapist helped me understand that my confining circumstances tapped into my core feelings of powerlessness and fear. To counteract these feelings, I'd go into an uncontrollable rage. She insisted I hire in-house help to prevent future out-of-control episodes and the risk of me hurting my children.

This was difficult for me to accept. Thoughts raced through my head—I'm a do-all, do it well, "super woman." Women in my church don't hire outside help, what would people think? What about the money?

I went home and told my husband of my counselor's advice. We decided we had to follow it. We hired a "mothers'-helper" for twenty hours each week for several months during this difficult stage of my recovery.

As I look back, I can say it was a very timely, wise decision. Although it cost us a lot financially, it was worth it because it gave me the time and freedom I needed to take care of myself, which immensely helped diffuse my rage.

A word about rage: rage is anger that is out of control. Rage can come upon you suddenly and without warning. Rage can be like a drug, engulfing you and causing you to act irresponsibly and dangerously. If you have experienced this deep and powerful level of anger, make a plan now to safeguard yourself, your children, and others. When rage threatens to take over:

1. Get away from others. If you have small children, put them in a safe place. If they are old enough, explain to them that Mom needs to be left alone for a while—that you are having some deep feelings you need to work through. Be sure to tell them that these feelings are not their fault and that they do not need to take care of you.

2. Calm yourself by breathing and counting to ten several times—I really mean several times.

3. Do some anger-release exercises to help diffuse the rage (see exercises at end of chapter).

4. If you still feel like hurting yourself or someone else, call an emergency hotline such as: Childhelp (1-800-4 ACHILD, Hearing Impaired 1-800-2 ACHILD). Organizations like this exist to help people anonymously with trained staff on a twenty-four-hour a day basis. There may also be some local crisis intervention organizations in

your area with similar services. Find the telephone numbers by looking them up in the Yellow Pages under Crisis Intervention. Keep these numbers handy for emergencies.

## Grief: The Healing Feelings

One day, after a very difficult morning, my feelings of worthlessness washed over me more powerfully then I had ever before felt them. I dropped to my knees and sobbed as I realized how really bad I felt inside—worthless, power-less, and very, very vulnerable. Through it all, I felt my Heavenly Father trying to comfort me.

Underneath my anger lay my sadness and the core of the abuse inflicted on me. My goal in recovery was to grieve in a way that enabled me to rebuild my self-worth, starting from the core of my pain and working outward. I allowed myself to mourn and weep for what I had lost. As a sur-vivor of sexual abuse, I had a lot to grieve for—the loss of self, the loss of innocence, the loss of pleasant, secure feel-ings. You may also need to grieve for your abandonment, for the loss of your Inner Child, for the loss of a family you thought you had, or for a childhood that was unhappy.

You will need to grieve for the time you have lost to the repression of your pain, for the opportunities lost to fear and self-doubt, for the relationships that have been hurt and possibly destroyed. You will need to grieve for the per-son you have never known because she was too afraid to be herself, to face the reality of her past. You will also have to grieve many spiritual losses. (For more help in how to deal with these, see Chapter 7, Spiritual Grief.)

I feel very strongly that by allowing ourselves to feel our grief and weep the tears of loss in a safe, supportive setting, we enhance and accelerate our healing experience. Your Inner Child needs to cry the tears she was never allowed so that she can validate her grief. Crying for and sharing your grief with others who are understanding and safe validates your reality and helps free you from the pain of your past.

Grief can be healed naturally if we have support. As my husband learned more and more about the healing process, he was more capable of offering me support and validation to help me heal my grief. Of this, Jane Middleton-Moz and Lorie Dwinell have said, "One of the things we know about grief resolution is that grief is one of the only problems in the world that will heal itself with support."[4]

You may be able to find support for your grief with safe family members, spouses, friends, and church leaders, although this is easier for some than for others. I think the best resource for grief support is usually a support group that can identify with your losses. (For suggestions on how to find and choose a support group, see Chapter 5.)

If you are like some survivors, you will find that crying does not come easily. It brings you too close to the pain you have been avoiding all of your life. If you find you cannot move past the anger, perhaps you are afraid of the feelings of grief. Please believe that crying helps you move into the core of your sadness, assisting you in the expression of your grief by moving the sadness and pain upward and out.

> *I sit here weeping, releasing the pain of my abuse. It is so good to finally let the pain out, to allow myself the tears and the anger of it. I am worthy of that, worthy of these feelings. I have always been worthy, but nobody ever taught me that I was. I am so thankful for what I now know. Knowledge is power.*
>
> —*A Survivor*

> *I am allowing my feelings to come and allowing myself to feel them. I am getting to the pain that lies beneath my strong anger. I now see the light at the end of the tunnel, which I didn't see a while ago. My*

*prayers are being heard and answered.*

*—A Survivor*

In Luke 6:21 we learn this: "Blessed are ye that weep now: for ye shall laugh." In Psalms 126:5 we are taught that "they that sow in tears shall reap in joy." In Romans 12:15 we are told to find support in our weeping: "Rejoice with them that do rejoice, and weep with them that weep." These scriptures share the same message: they tell us that allowing ourselves to cry with others will relieve us of a tremendous emotional weight, making room for feelings of joy, peace, and happiness. We have been promised that the Savior will aid us in our grief: "For the Lamb which is in the midst of the throne shall feed them, and shall lead them unto living fountains of waters: and God shall wipe away all tears from their eyes" (Revelation 7:17).

One night I turned to my husband and said that I needed to talk. I asked him to hold me as I told him some of the experiences I had gone through—not all—just those that I'd been thinking about that day. I shuddered and cried as I spoke. He didn't always know what to say, but he learned to say "I can see you are in a lot of pain and I validate your pain." He told me he believed what I shared, and never challenged it. He told me he believed me and loved me.

You will know you are beginning to heal when you begin to talk about your pain more comfortably and once again start experiencing the full range of human emotions.

## The Work of Feeling

Allowing myself to once again feel was hard work, especially in the beginning of my recovery. Feeling my feelings was physically and emotionally draining. There were days when I was unable to perform normal tasks. This was particularly difficult for me because the work ethic is especially strong in religious sub-cultures such as mine. We've learned to equate personal value with work.

But just because the work of learning to feel can't be *seen* doesn't mean you are having a non-productive day. During the first stages of recovery, I needed to devote a lot of time and energy to feeling. Some days it seemed like all I did was sit and feel. Doing anything more than that seemed impossible. During this difficult time, I gave myself credit for working hard all day on feeling and remembering, on taking care of my Inner Child. I gave myself credit for taking care of myself in a way that kept me from hitting my son, screaming at my daughter, swearing at my husband, or going into an uncontrollable rage. You, too, can give yourself credit for allowing yourself to feel bad and to grieve inwardly and outwardly.

Because I was willing to experience a full range of emotions, I allowed the pain to come to a point in my life that I realized how bad I really felt about myself. Allowing this to happen stripped away all the facades—the "doings" did not work any more. All the addictions and "doings" that I had used to mask my pain had been stripped from me. The core of me was exposed. This allowed me to be in a position to start rebuilding. At times when I was dealing with my biggest wounds, pains, and shame-based feelings, I felt that I might not get back on my feet, that I was a victim and I had been beaten down. I wondered if I would own any strengths again in my personality and character, but, I did get back on my feet again and so can you.

Emotion is energy in motion. Your repressed feelings are blocked energy that needs to be released. Choose to release this energy by allowing yourself to feel your feelings. Please don't worry about fixing them, changing them, or getting rid of them. Allowing yourself to simply feel your feelings will allow the energy of your emotions to be released.

There is no special order to the work of feeling your feelings. For some survivors numbness comes first; for others it is anger; for others it is sadness, sorrow, and tears. All you really need to do is keep your feelings in motion by expressing your emotional energy in safe ways and in safe places. As I appropriately released the powerful emotion locked inside of me, I fully believed that I needed to experience and manage my feelings.

The exercises listed below can help you appropriately release the powerful emotion locked inside of you.

**1. Body Feelings.** When attempting to allow your feelings to emerge, pay attention to your body. Breathe deeply and slowly and tell your body to relax. When you are trying to dissociate from a feeling, your body may tighten and constrict in certain areas. There were many times when I would just sit and allow my body to feel my feelings. I would tell myself, "All I have to do right now is sit and feel, and everything will be okay."

**2. Recovery Journal.** Write how you are feeling in a journal. Some survivors fear their journals will be discovered and read by others. It is not wise to leave your journal laying around—be sure to put it in a secure place. I kept a journal all through my recovery. I found it to be powerfully therapeutic to write about how I felt. I still prefer to keep this type of journal verses a log of events. I need a safe place to express myself, and my journal offers me that experience.

**3. Music.** Express your feelings with music. You can find music to fit every mood. When I felt discouraged and needed to feel strength and the will to keep going, I would play certain songs. When I felt success and genuine healing, I had other songs that I played to celebrate the positive changes occurring in my life. I found that music validated my feelings and I would use it to keep me going. Find songs that create those same feelings of validation for you. Play them often.

**4. Art Therapy.** Using a piece of paper and crayons, express yourself by drawing your feelings. Draw free form, with no specific idea in mind; just draw as you feel. Use shapes, color, and degrees of pressure to form pictures that have special meanings to you. Draw your pain, what it looks like to you. Draw your shame, your anger. Draw any of the feelings you are experiencing. Each feeling will look different. Then draw the way you want to feel. Share these drawings with a supportive and trusted friend. If you are seeing a therapist, show this person what you have drawn, and talk about how you are now feeling and how you want to feel.

**5. Anger Release Work.** When your anger is triggered and you sense it rising up, take time to deal with it. Give yourself permission to be angry. The following can help in either situation:

- **Dish Toss.** Purchase some old dishes at a thrift shop. Take them to a place where you can throw them without damaging walls or floors, and where you can be alone. (The corner of an unfinished basement is a great place!) Put on some complementary music and fling away. With each toss of a dish express something that you are mad about.

- **Exercise.** If you like to exercise, get out there and do it when you're upset. Put five miles under your feet, pushing your anger into your muscles and out of your glands as you sweat. Work out on a step machine or exercise bike. Pretend you are kicking your abuser when you do aerobics. I guarantee you'll get a great workout.

- **Physical Release.** Punch, hit, or tear something. Scream at the same time. Be sure you do it in a safe way, in a safe place. Go to your bedroom and punch pillows, tear an old sheet into tiny pieces, whack your tennis racket onto the mattress of your bed, put your head into your pillow and scream. The point here is not to destroy, but to release energy generated by anger.

- **Letter Writing.** Write letters to your abuser, your parents, family members, and anyone else who has hurt you. Tell each person what you are angry about. Tell them what your Inner Child needed that she didn't get. Tell them how mad you are about what they did to you and how their actions have damaged your life.

  Because these letters will probably be charged with a high level of emotion, I recommend letter-writing be used as a release rather than for correspondence. If you are considering sending a letter, ask yourself first, "Will sending this letter help me more than hurt me?" Your second question should be, "Am I ready to deal with the actions and words of those I am sending the letters to?" If the answer is "no" to either question, do not mail the letters.

- **Visualizations.** In a visualization exercise, go to your Inner Child and invite her to come with you to have a meeting with your abuser. Ask her if she wants anyone else to come with her to protect and help her. Explain that you would like her to express her angry feelings to your abuser. Reassure her that she will not be harmed; you will not allow it. Visually see yourself and your Inner Child confronting the abuser, and encourage her to tell the abuser how he has hurt her. Let her know it is okay to be angry at the abuser.

1. Louise M. Wisechild, *The Obsidian Mirror: An Adult Healing from Incest.* Seattle, Washington: The Seal Press, 1988.

2. Parley P. Pratt, *Key to the Science of Theology*, p. 101.

3. Laura Davis and Ellen Bass, *The Courage to Heal,* (New York: Harper and Row, 1988), p. 127.

4. Jane Middleton-Moz and Lorie Dwinell. *After the Tears.* Deerfield Beach, Florida: Health Communications, Inc., 1986.

# CHAPTER 4
## RECLAIMING AND EMBRACING YOUR WOUNDED INNER CHILD

*My child inside of me is crying—crying the tears that were never allowed all through my childhood. There is a lot of pain, and sometimes I wonder if it will ever go away, The pain I buried along with my child self so many years ago. As a child I was forced to hold my head high and bury the pain, just to carry on.*

*I must learn to let the tears of my childhood flow to wash and cleanse the pain of my past. I must allow my Inner Child to grieve the damage that was done to her. I must now take care of my wounded Inner Child and never leave her alone again.*

—*A Survivor*

Reading such thoughts changed my life; they spoke truth to me and allowed me to start remembering, reclaiming, and embracing my wounded Inner Child. When I read this passage for the first time, I felt that my Inner Child who had been hurt and abandoned so long ago finally had a voice to speak, and I was ready and willing to listen.

This chapter will teach you philosophies and techniques regarding what is referred to as "Inner Child work." During my recovery I felt impressed to learn about this type of treatment. I went to John Bradshaw's workshops and read his books, as well as books written by Alice Miller, Charles Whitfield, and other authors. (See Recovery Resource in the appendix for information on these authors' books.) This chapter combines ideas that have been adapted from these authors' work with ideas of my own.

Healing my Inner Child was a critical step in coming to full and complete recovery. Nevertheless, many treatment philosophies are available to us today in addition to the Inner Child work. Through the power of prayer and the guidance of the Holy Ghost, you will know which will be right for you.

You now have the opportunity as I did to free yourself from the abuse of your childhood by introducing your adult self to your child self of long ago. You need to travel back through your conscious and subconscious mind to the memory of your pain. You will feel your feelings, grieve your losses, meet your unmet needs, heal your wounds, and finish any unfinished business of your past.

> *The pain can erupt when it is triggered, so I must cry to wash and cleanse the pain of my past. I must grieve the damage that was done. I must allow myself to carry on and make my future better.*
> —*A Survivor*

### Who is Your Inner Child?

There are many names and descriptions in the world of psychotherapy that describe the Inner Child. Charles Whitfield refers to this child as the "Child Within," describing her as "that part of us which is ultimately alive, energetic, creative, and fulfilled; it is our Real Self—who we truly are." [1]

Some authors refer to this child as the "wonder child." Still others call this part of our being the Real Self, Inner Self, Inner Vessel, Spirit Self, Core Self, Divine Child, Inner World, Inner Life, Life Within, Higher Self, and Spirit Being.

All these terms refer to who we really are in the core of our being—the most vital and spontaneous part of us. Your Inner Child is smart and sensitive, nurturing and caring, powerful and wise, lovable and capable. Members of the LDS Church would say that the Inner Child is the spirit self, the true "spirit child of God."

I consider it spiritual abuse whenever this inner spirit self is wounded or when abuse damages spiritual development.

Any form of child abuse hinders the development of your core self, your spirit self. It masks your ability to feel your own worth and connectedness to God.

Chinese philosophy teaches that the Inner Child holds in balance all the qualities of Yin and Yang. She is a sensible, lively, spunky individual with a great desire to live life to the fullest. But she can't be free to express herself unless she is rescued from her abuse, until she feels and knows for certain that she is safe.

In the Parable of the Lost Sheep, I believe Christ shares some powerful insights about child abuse. The lost sheep in this parable is usually interpreted as someone going astray from the gospel or from his or her values in adult life. We have been correctly taught that each soul is important to God, and have been admonished to help those who have strayed from the straight and narrow path that returns us to God. Spiritual healing is about recovering from spiritual abuse.

Because I lost my Inner Child early and then found her later in my life, the Parable of the Lost Sheep has a different meaning for me personally.

Take heed that ye despise not one of these little ones; for I say unto you, That in heaven their angels do always behold the face of my Father which is in heaven.

For the Son of man is come to save that which was lost.

How think ye? if a man have an hundred sheep, and one of them be gone astray, doth he not leave the ninety and nine, and goeth into the mountains, and seeketh that which is gone astray?

And if so be that he find it, verily I say unto you, he rejoiceth more of that sheep, than of the ninety and nine which went not astray.

Even so it is not the will of your Father which is in heaven, that one of these little ones should perish. (Matthew 18:10-14.)

Both before and after Christ teaches us about his "lost sheep," he refers to little children. We should not "despise" little children, he tells us, for they have "angels" who watch over them in behalf of Heavenly Father. He then teaches us about the lost sheep. I believe this lost child exists within abuse survivors, and this is our own "lost sheep." This is the child who is abandoned and lost when she is abused, sexually or otherwise.

I believe that we do not choose to lose our child self; we lose her in order to survive the abuse. Little children do not choose to go astray. They grow up and become adults who go astray because they became lost. And how did they become lost? I suppose the same way I did. I lost the connection with my soul when I abandoned my wounded Inner Child, covering up my real divine self with a false self, because I believed that my real abused self was bad.

We learn in the Parable of the Lost Sheep that Christ came to earth and died for us to save each of our souls, the

Inner Children, the divine real selves of men and women. "For the Son of man is come to save that which is lost" (Matthew 18:11). Heavenly Father does not want us to perish; he wants to help us rescue the child we abandoned long ago. Christ will aid you, just as he aided me, in your quest to find your wounded Inner Child and to heal her.

In the beginning of your recovery from sexual or other abuse, your Inner Child is not yet free to positively influence your life with all her wisdom and power. Trapped within her, within you, are all her feelings of shame, worthlessness, powerlessness, guilt, and fear. She may currently be influencing your life in a negative way because she is still trying to protect herself from being hurt, shamed, and abandoned again. John Bradshaw teaches us that "if our vulnerable child was hurt or abandoned, shamed or neglected, that child's pain, grief, and anger live on within us."[2]

Your Inner Child believes she has to take care of herself—even at the expense of both you and others—because nobody else is taking care of her. Addictions are one of the most powerful tools she often uses for protection. They offer a false and temporary sense of happiness and security. John Bradshaw tells us that "addiction has become our national lifestyle (or rather death style)." This is a . . . "death style based on the relinquishment of the self as a worthwhile being to a self who must achieve and perform or use something outside of self in order to be lovable and happy."[3]

Your wounded Inner Child may push you toward all kinds of excesses in her effort to feel better. For example, overeating makes the Inner Child feel full and drugs mask her emotional and physical pain. Overachieving in school, work, or church positions gives her praise and validation from others. Extensive to-do lists make her feel more in control of her life. Obesity protects her from her shamed sexuality. Excessive neatness and cleanliness counteract the dirtiness she feels about herself. Anger and rage give her a sense of power. Submissiveness and co-dependency make her feel needed. Silence and withdrawal protect her from being hurt. I found that these and other addictions were counterfeit remedies, which offered substitute feelings that were short-term and guilt producing. My addictions only stifled my free agency because they limited my power to choose what was best for me at a given moment.

I struggled with an eating disorder as a teenager. When I turned sixteen, I gained a lot of weight due to my uncontrollable binging. I felt such a powerful sense of worthlessness and emptiness that I turned to food in an attempt to fill up this huge empty hole in myself. I really lost control. All this just added to my core feelings of shame and worthlessness.

As a result of my childhood abuse, my Inner Child felt completely worthless. In order for her to feel any sense of value, I became an obsessive overachiever in my adult life. I became addicted to "superhuman doings"; everything I did had to be perfect. I had it figured out that I needed to be superhuman, because "less than nothing plus superhuman averages out to be nearly adequate."

My wounded Inner Child was desperately alone and isolated. I was operating with false beliefs, my core belief being that I deserved every bad thing that happened to me because I WAS BAD. The truth of the matter was that I was not bad. I WAS WOUNDED. My Inner Child had been abandoned internally and externally, isolated with her feelings of shame. She had been robbed and injured.

She was "snared in holes, and [she was] hid in prison houses: [she was] for a prey, and none delivereth; for a spoil, and none saith, Restore" (Isaiah 42:22).

This scripture suggests to me that because of the trauma of child sexual abuse, I felt I had to hide my real self, my

Inner Child from further pain. As an adult survivor, I knew it was now my opportunity, my divine task to heal the wounds of my past and re-parent my Inner Child. This enabled me to restore true feelings of empowerment, self-love, and divinity to my inner self.

Christ said "Be ye therefore perfect" (Matthew 5:48), not "do ye therefore perfect." We are to be perfect in our *beings*, not in our *doings*. As children we learned to mirror our earthly parents. Many of us therefore need to work through all the shame we soaked in as children that causes us to believe that we are bad. As adults we need to heal our Inner Child which then allows us to mirror our Heavenly Parents and become whole. Then we can realize that we are perfect creations because our Father in Heaven is perfect and He created perfection. However, the footnote for Matthew 5:48 "Be ye therefore perfect," tells us that the word "perfect" was translated from the Greek word that means complete, finished, fully developed. We simply are not expected to be complete, finished, or fully developed at any certain moment of our lives, but can only be perfectly fulfilling his plan of progress for us. This kind of progress brings peace. *Perfectionism,* or trying to *appear* and *do* everything perfect *now,* brings torment, not peace.

> *I believed I had been in control of my life when in reality my dependencies and addictions had really been controlling me. I let go of my inner self, my Inner Child, and gave in to my dependencies and addictions, which were literally my gods. I had placed my faith and trust in my addictions and dependencies and not in Christ.*
>
> *I distrusted myself, my judgment, my decisions, my mind, my life, and my ability to be on my own without my dependencies and addictions. I distrusted my bishops, my parents, people in the church. My*

*distrust moved into fear. I became fear based. My
foundation in life was fear.*

*I was afraid I was dying. I was afraid I could not
keep the surface looking good; I had to keep up the
superhuman doings. I was so worthless. I was nothing,
I was non-existent and I had no value.*

*I prayed, I pleaded, I begged, I cried, I felt tor-
mented. I went in prayer to my Heavenly Father
asking for his help. Asking for the direction of the
Holy Ghost in my life. Knowing that fear and faith
cannot co-exist, I asked myself how I could change
my fear to faith.*

*I admitted I was powerless, that I was defeated,
that there was something wrong in my life. I told my
Heavenly Father I could longer control my life, that
I was in darkness and in pain, that I was really suffering. This I knew at last was my reality.*

*—A Survivor*

## How to Develop a Relationship with Your Inner Child

The first step in connecting with your wounded Inner
Child is to believe and validate her story of abuse. She is in
isolation because she has had nowhere to go to share her pain.

I had frozen the reality of my abuse because I feared that
if I shared it I would not be believed; I would be shamed
and abandoned. As a child, one of my greatest fears was
abandonment.

I wanted so much to find someone I could tell, someone
who would believe me and validate me. I needed to be
heard and believed. Through my recovery process, however, I've learned that it is most important to hear ourselves, believe ourselves, and to believe *in* ourselves.

You must tell yourself now that you will not abandon
your Inner Child. This takes great courage and strength.

Coming into an intimate relationship with yourself as a child means you are willing to hear and feel the depth of her pain and face all of her terror. It means remembering a time when you did not have the power to protect yourself. It means acknowledging any and all abuse—it really did happen. It is very likely that you will be the first person to believe and validate your Inner Child.

Perhaps you do not want a relationship with your child self at this time. You may blame her for what happened to you as a child. You may hate her for being so small, for being needy and vulnerable, for allowing the abuse to happen. Please realize that your neediness as a child helped make you vulnerable to victimization.

Think of yourself as the vulnerable child you were, possibly six years old or even younger. Think of how little you were, of how much you needed love and hugs, and how you longed to be held. Some people may ask, "Why didn't you tell someone?" making you feel responsible for not taking better care of yourself at such an early age.

I asked the little child inside of me, "Why didn't you tell? Why didn't you get help?"

Here are some of the answers she gave me, along with some answers other survivors have given:

- I wasn't absolutely sure anything was wrong. (Remember the confusion when the enemy isn't clearly defined.)
- I didn't know who to tell and didn't think anyone would believe me.
- I did tell and no one believed me.
- I was too ashamed; I even felt it was my fault.
- I was too frightened to say anything because I was told bad things would happen if I told.

Your abuser may have scared you into silence with threats like these:

- If you tell, I will kill you.

- If you tell, you'll be sent away.
- If you tell, I won't love you anymore.
- If you tell, God won't love you.
- If you tell, it will kill your mother.
- If you tell, no one will believe you or love you anymore.

Some threats were very real to me when I was a child. My Inner Child still believed they were real because no one had made the commitment to protect her. My Inner Child was anxiously waiting for me to assure her safety now. Nonetheless, I still had to win her trust.

You need to do as I did, to tell your Inner Child that she is safe now because you are here to protect her. Do not be surprised if she does not believe you; she may not be ready to trust you yet. You have repressed your memories and feelings, ignoring her all these years, so it may take some time to win her trust.

Some of the exercises that follow helped me get in touch with my Inner Child:

**1. Childhood Pictures.** Find several pictures of yourself in various stages of your childhood. Look at these pictures often. Carry your favorite one in your wallet or recovery journal. I was able to find several pictures of myself from infancy through adolescence. They helped me recall what I looked like as a child at different ages and reminded me to nurture my Inner Child.

**2. Letter Writing.** One of the most powerful tools for getting in touch with my Inner Child and discovering how she felt was to write letters to her. With my dominant hand I would write a letter to "Little Carol" from "Big Carol," asking her questions like, "How are you feeling? What are you scared of? How do you feel about your father? How do you feel about your mother?" As the relationship got safer for both of us, I asked for more painful information, "Tell me about your abuse. Tell me about the greatest pains of your childhood." I would then write back as "Little Carol," using my non-dominant hand to mimic a child's writing. My letters would begin with "Dear Big Carol," and end with "Love, Little Carol." This exercise revealed some of my most powerful feelings that I'd never expressed as a child.

**3. Writing Exercises.** To help you understand that your being is whole and that the abuse was not your fault, write the following sentences (or create your own to fit your needs). Write them twenty to thirty times, using your non-dominant hand. Repeat this exercise as needed throughout your recovery to work through feelings of blame and guilt.

I, Little (put in your name), am whole and flawless.

The abuse was not my fault.

I was small and innocent.

To learn about what you were like as a child, finish incomplete sentences like the following, again using your non-dominant hand:

I am . . .

I feel . . .

I fear . .

I hate . . .

I like . . .

I feel safe when . . .

I don't feel safe when . . .

I feel bad when . . .

I feel good when . . .

One thing I would really like to do is . . .

**4. Visualization Exercises.** Visualization exercises are another powerful tool for connecting with your Inner Child. Create a safe place in your mind where you can meet with your child often. This can be a beautiful room or a beautiful place in nature where you meet your child. In my visualizations I go down a hall to a room that I have created. The room is all white and filled with big comfortable furniture. One wall of the room is all windows that look out to the ocean and the beach, where I can see the power of the waves. In this room I meet with my Inner Child, take care of her, talk to her, and encourage her to talk to me. If I want to take my Inner Child outside into nature, I exit through the door and go further down the hall, up some stairs, and through another door, which opens to a beautiful hillside in the country.

To help you introduce yourself to your Inner Child and to develop a relationship with the Savior in your healing, I have included at the end of this chapter a visualization exercise written by another survivor, a good friend of mine. If you relate to it, you may want to record it on tape and listen to it repeatedly. I recommend Steven Halpren's meditation music for the Inner Child as background music.

## Parenting Your Wounded Inner Child

Once you have connected with your Inner Child, you need to begin re-parenting her in order to liberate her and integrate her into your life. There were many things I needed as a child that I didn't get. I needed to be held and loved unconditionally, not shamed and abandoned. There were many things I needed to learn in order to feel a sense of empowerment and individuality. After having children of my own I realized that—like all children—my own greatest need as an infant and small child was love. I took what I could get, even when it was not the real thing.

I also realized the developmental stages of my childhood had been arrested. John Bradshaw teaches us that "each developmental stage is unique with its own special needs and dynamics."[4]

I discovered that when these developmental needs were not met in my childhood, I went through life trying to get other people to parent me and meet my needs. But other people couldn't take care of me that way. They didn't know my needs or have the capacity to heal me. I didn't even know my own needs myself until I started healing. Because I grew up with a false self, leaving my child self behind, I developed ego defenses that were critical for my emotional survival. The defenses that helped me survive as a child became barriers to my growth as an adult.

I also learned that as an adult I had the power to choose to let go of these barriers by meeting the unmet needs of my Inner Child. I had the power to validate myself and to subconsciously reshape my past to empower and individualize my child. Once I had connected my child self to my adult self, I could lead my child self to the perfect source of healing, Jesus Christ.

Parenting myself and taking my child to Christ to receive his light and love created a safer place for my subconscious mind (Inner Child) to reveal itself. Being nurtured by the Savior accelerated my healing. Nobody else healed me or took care of my Inner Child's needs as well as the Savior and I did. My empowerment came by learning to heal myself with the Savior's help. Here are some of the exercises I found helpful in re-parenting my Inner Child:

1. **Affirmations.** During your infancy and childhood you needed to hear words like "You are so important to me. I'm glad you are here." You can now do this for yourself or have someone you trust affirm you. During my recovery I attended a workshop where the facilitator organized us into groups of six. One by one each of us took a turn sitting in the middle of the group. We told the others if we were comfortable with gentle touching or hugs. After we set our boundaries, each of the others communicated verbal

affirmations to us as we sat in the middle. This brought powerful emotional responses from us. To finally hear the things we did not hear as children was deeply healing.

To affirm your Inner Child, this exercise can be done with a support group or by using your own visualizations. Here are some suggested verbal affirmations for children of different ages that I tried. (If you are a parent, hold your own children and verbally affirm them. You will be amazed how eager they are to hear your words.)

## Infant

- I'm glad you were born.
- You deserved to be born.
- I'm so happy to be your mother/father.
- I want to take care of you.
- Your body is so healthy and beautiful.
- I'm glad you're a girl/boy.
- I love you.

## Toddler

- I like you just the way you are.
- I will never leave you.
- It's okay to cry and to be angry—I will not go away.
- You're more important than a clean house.
- It's okay for you to say, "No."
- It's okay for you to get dirty and messy.

## Youngster (school age)

- The problems in the family are not your fault.
- You don't need to take care of me. I will take care of you.
- I want you to be truly you.
- It's okay to make mistakes.

- Mistakes help you learn.
- I love you just the way you are.
- I'm willing to be with you no matter what you are feeling.

**2. Reshaping the Past.** Visualize your adult self taking the police with you to arrest your molester. After the police have taken the abuser away, take your child self and hold her in your arms. Tell her you've come to protect her and you're not going to let this happen anymore. Keep reminding her that you are now the one taking care of her. In one of my visualizations, I saw my adult self using martial arts to restrain the perpetrator, then I handed him over to the police who took him to jail, where he could never again hurt my child self. If you desire, you could have your adult self be the one to get rid of your abuser and rescue your child. Doing this for your Inner Child will build feelings of trust and love. I found that these exercises added power and strength to my child self and allowed me to go as an adult to my child to rescue her.

Another option is to give more of the power to your Inner Child. See the room where the abuse took place. See the perpetrator. See your Inner Child push him away, saying, "No, get away from me. I won't let you do this to me. If you don't stop, I will scream and I will tell." Visualize the perpetrator running away from you, getting smaller and smaller as he/she runs off.

When I finish a visualization and it's time for me to leave my Inner Child, I invite Heavenly Father to take care of her for me until I return. Sometimes I even visualize a loving heavenly mother and ask her to stay with my Inner Child.

Studies have shown that visualizations like these have a permanent influence on our subconscious. Our minds respond to the new memory we have created, giving us genuine feelings of empowerment and worth.

**3. Reclaiming Your Child.** In a visualization, go to one of your childhood homes and find your Inner Child. Tell her you have come to take her with you. She may already have her bags packed ready to go, or she may not want to go. If the latter is the case, tell her it's okay if she's not ready to go; you want to meet her needs. Explain to her that you are her new parent and you have come to take care of her. Tell her you will wait until she is ready to leave. Tell her she does not have to earn your protection, that you will give it freely. Ask her what she needs and what you can do to make her feel safe. When she's ready, take her with you, leaving your childhood home behind.

This exercise establishes a precedent: you are now the one in charge of taking care of your child and your own life.

## How Inner Child Work Will Help You Heal Your Way to Happiness

Reclaiming and embracing your wounded Inner Child will allow you to make deep and lasting changes. Nurturing and parenting your Inner Child will lead you to a creative and lasting relationship with yourself. Spending ten minutes a day with your child self equals hours in our adult time; there is no time frame in our subconscious. You may have to repeat exercises and remind your child that things are different now. Think of how many times a child needs to be taught the same ideas over and over again.

As a result of doing this work, I found a deep and abiding love for my child self, and an inner peace. It was only through my real self, my core being, my Inner Child, that I learned to love myself and receive the love of Christ. I believe this is why we've been told to become as little children. Moroni tells us that "little children are whole"

(Moroni 8:8). Our child selves are real, genuine, and whole.

> At the same time came the disciples unto Jesus, saying, Who is the greatest in the kingdom of heaven?
> And Jesus called a little child unto him, and set him in the midst of them,
> And said, Verily I say unto you, Except ye be converted, and become as little children, ye shall not enter into the kingdom of heaven.
> Whosoever therefore shall humble himself as this little child, the same is greatest in the kingdom of heaven.
> And whoso shall receive one such little child in my name receiveth me. (Matthew 18:1-5.)

When Heavenly Father asks each of us to become as a little child, I believe he is asking us to become whole by receiving and healing our Inner Child. A little child is pure and whole, without blemish or shame. The process of becoming as a little child is the process of becoming sanctified, of becoming holy and whole. It should be our life's journey to find the wholeness that lies within our being. Reclaiming and embracing my Inner Child started me on the journey to recovery. It is my belief the process I have just described will work for you.

## Taking Your Inner Child To Christ

Betty Holland, a certified guided imagery counselor, is gifted in teaching survivors how to use age regression therapy in healing their Inner Child. She wrote this powerful visualization to help survivors take their Inner Child to Christ to be healed.

Get in a relaxed position. Sitting or lying down is okay. Close your eyes and breathe deeply. Take ten to fifteen deep breaths. While you are breathing, let all the thoughts in your mind float away. Keep breathing deeply. Remember, let the worries of your day float out of your mind. If thoughts come back into your mind, let them in then let them float away. Don't worry about this. Just relax. As you are breathing, relax your neck . . . relax your shoulders . . . relax your feet . . . and your toes. Keep breathing and let the thoughts float away. Picture yourself as you want to become. If you have trouble with this, just think about seeing yourself and continue to relax and breathe. Think about the person you want to become. See yourself in this wonderful vision. Now take yourself and walk on the path that is in front of you. Create a beautiful place in nature where you really like to be. Continue to walk on the path. Notice the beauty. Notice the trees . . . the plants . . . the birds. Hear the birds. Smell the wild flowers. Notice how peaceful it is. Notice how peaceful you feel. Enjoy your walk and the peace. While you are walking, look up and see in front of you a beautiful meadow. In this meadow you see a child sitting a few yards away. Walk up to this child. As you approach this child, you can see this little child is you. You go up to this little child and tell her you are so happy to meet her. You want to spend some time with her. You have been missing her and have been wanting to be with her. You tell her you are now her mother. You now want to take care of her. You now want to be with her and build trust between you. You want her to decide to do something she has always wanted to do as a child but never got to do. (It is very important that you share this event with your child.) When your child decides what she wants to do, tell your child you want to be with her and help her do this event, and you want to share this event with her. Tell your child you want to get to know her better. Take your child by the hand and go and do this event she has always wanted to do. (Two-minute pause.) Tell your child it will be time to go in a minute. (Thirty-second pause.) It is time to go. Take your child by the hand and leave this wonderful event. As you leave, get back on the path and walk together. Notice this beautiful place in nature as you walk. Share this with your child and tell her how much you enjoyed being with her today, how much you enjoyed sharing her life for a while. While you walk with her, look up and see a door and a room ahead of you. Walk up to the door and open it. This room is your room and your Inner Child's room. Decorate the room any way you want. This is a special room just for you and your Inner Child. Maybe it has a lot of windows, plants, beautiful draperies, books, furniture, soft sofa and chairs, whatever you like. Let your child have what she wants in this room also. (Two-minute pause.) When you finish decorating this room, spend time there with your child. Just sit with your child. Rock your child. Read to your child. Just hold your child. Share kind words with your child. Maybe your child wants to tell you something. Just quietly listen. whatever your child needs or wants. (Two-minute pause.) It is time to go in a minute. Let your child get ready to go. Take her hand. Get up.

Walk over to the door. Open the door. Walk out
of the room on to the path. Take the path that
goes through nature. Walk together over by the
stream. Enjoy the beauty, the rushing water, the
birds, the flowers, the peace. This has been a
good day. Enjoy this time. Look up and see Jesus
sitting on a log in a cluster of trees by the stream.
Walk over to Jesus and let your child be with
Jesus for a few minutes. Maybe your child has
something to tell Jesus. Maybe she wants to tell
Jesus about her day. Maybe she wants to be held
by Jesus. Maybe she wants to be in the presence
of Jesus. Whatever your child wants and needs at
this time, let her receive. (One-minute pause.)
Maybe your adult self needs to be with Jesus and
receive from him . . . whatever you want. You and
your Inner Child be there with Jesus. (One-
minute pause.) It is time to leave. Ask your child
if she wants to stay with Jesus or if she wants to
come with you. Let your child decide. If she
wants to stay with Jesus that is okay. Assure your
Inner Child you will be back again to visit or to
come and get her. If your child wants to come
with you, take her by the hand to leave, but
before leaving be sure to thank Jesus for spending
time with you and express your appreciation to
Him. Take your child's hand and walk away. Get
back on the path you started on. Tell your Inner
Child (if she is with you) that this was a wonderful day to be with her. As you walk on the path,
put your arm around your child and bring her
close to you and pull your child into you as you
become ONE. Continue on the path with yourself. You are now coming back where you started.
Notice the chair you are in. Feel the chair you are

in. Move your legs, your fingers, your toes, your
arms. Open your eyes when you are ready.


1. Charles Whitfield, *Healing the Child Within.* Deerfield
Beach, Florida: Health Communications, Inc., 1987, p. 1.
2. John Bradshaw, *Homecoming: Reclaiming and
Championing Your Inner Child.* New York: Bantam Books,
1990, Jacket Cover. (A concise and thorough description of
what your developmental dependency needs were as a child
and how you can meet them as an adult.)
3. John Bradshaw, *Bradshaw on the Family.* (Deerfield
Beach, Florida: Health Communications, Inc., 1988), p. 6.
4. John Bradshaw, *Healing the Shame That Binds You.*
Deerfield Beach, Florida: Health Communications, Inc.,
1988, p.139.

# CHAPTER 5
## BREAKING THE SILENCE:
## A SAFE PLACE TO TALK

*Unless the Lord had been my help, my soul had almost dwelt in silence.*
*—Psalms 94:17*

Sharing my story of abuse in a confidential, safe setting—and having it validated—was essential to my recovery. I knew that healing from child sexual abuse was too much to handle alone; trying to heal while perpetuating that lonely silence was impossible. I needed to find, or create, a safe place to share my feelings with others who believed and supported me—a safe place where I could feel protected while I built the skills that allowed me to remember my abuse, validate my feelings, and heal the pain of my past. Deep healing could occur when I told my story in a safe place because I could share my feelings instead of having to explain or justify myself.

I was reliving devastating events, and until I had established a support system, I felt alone and unprepared to deal with my memories. As time went by, I remembered still more horrible events, but facing my reality became easier, because I had found support and was able to talk about it. I was able to get it out in front of me where I could see it—by talking about it. Talking about my abuse helped me to establish myself as a person in the here and now dealing with abuse in my past. I came to realize that what had happened to me was not my fault, nor was it a statement about who I was.

Uninformed people may say to you, "That happened such a long time ago. Just forget about it and move on with your life. Why are you bringing this up now? Forget the past and look to the future. If you keep going over it, you'll get stuck in it. Just think about the positive and you'll be happy. We all have bad things happen to us, but we don't have to dwell on them. Just leave the bad things behind." A positive mental attitude is a great thing to have, but it will not heal the wounds of an abusive childhood. One survivor shares how she felt when confronted with comments like those above.

> *I desire to deal with my life in a realistic way. I do this by seeking to know and understand my past. Receiving and offering support to others helps me to gain strength, to overcome the negatives, and to learn and apply gospel principles that will aid me in rebuilding and reshaping my future.*
>
> —*A Survivor*

In Ecclesiastes 3:7 we are taught that there is "a time to keep silence, and a time to speak." As a survivor, you need to learn when it's in your best interest to keep silent and when it's safe to speak about your abuse. At the beginning of your recovery, you may feel a need to tell whomever will listen, or you may feel like you cannot share with anyone. I have learned to share with caution and that what I needed to share couldn't be received by just anyone.

You may be fortunate enough to have spiritual and ecclesiastical leaders who can understand the depth of your pain, or friends who can offer you support, but perhaps not—you may not even feel safe to share the reality of your abuse with your spouse yet. You are dealing with an issue that many people don't want to hear about, and their opinion is often "You just don't talk about it." Sharing your experience and pain with others who are not prepared to support you will hinder your recovery because you will once again feel rejected and shamed by their negative responses. You have a right to acknowledge your abuse, but don't look to individuals who are in denial for permission to heal.

Sharing your story at a church meeting or during an auxiliary lesson, unless you are invited to do so, can leave you feeling shamed and publicly discredited. Hearing stories of abuse tends to leave most listeners with negative feelings; for some, it may trigger painful feelings associated with their own unresolved abuse issues. When your listeners see you and remember, they may blame you for their pain since they don't know what to do with their feelings. Some listeners may even judge you and perceive you as a bad person, which may cause you again to feel victimized. This is because many people don't understand abuse or grief and don't know how to grieve for themselves, let alone grieve with or for others.

Before I was invited to speak about recovery, I shared my tragedy at a church meeting. It wasn't received. I learned that I need to protect the intimacies of my life by not sharing with others who may not be ready to receive it.

Ask your Heavenly Father to guide you in knowing when it's "time to keep silence" and when it's "time to speak." I've since been invited to speak about recovery in several church settings. But these have been meetings where the people have come to learn specifically about abuse. Before speaking I always ask Heavenly Father to help me to know how much I should share about myself and that I might convey a feeling of hope. Because I've trusted in the Holy Ghost to guide me in knowing what is safe and appropriate for me to share with the audience, each time I have spoken I have shared different things. God knows my audience more intimately then I do, so I trust God's judgment. This has protected me from the judgment of those who do not understand. I believe I am worth taking care of; with God's guidance, I can protect my Inner Child from feeling shamed and rejected again.

We are fortunate to live in a time when God has given us resources and tools to aid us in recovery from abuse. In my own and others' recovery, I have seen how a good therapist and a confidential support-group experience can be two of the most valuable means of support. A good therapist is a facilitator and teacher of healing, and a confidential support group can offer you validation and support—even become a substitute family for you to rely upon.

You are the only one who can know when you've found a therapist you are comfortable with and a support group in which you can feel safe. As in all other aspects of your recovery, please know that you can turn to your Father in Heaven through prayer and ask Him to guide you in your search. In my deepest pain I pled with Heavenly Father to guide me in finding some help. I was led to a great therapist and to a support group of LDS women who met weekly. You may find help quickly and easily, or you may need to shop around and try some different options before you find what is right for you.

## Finding and Choosing a Therapist: Some Guidelines

To gather names of therapists:

- Ask for referrals from other survivors who are or have been in therapy and were satisfied with their experience.
- Ask for referrals from your church leaders who are familiar

with the issues of abuse and who support the need for counseling.

- Call local hospitals, doctors, or nonprofit organizations that aid abuse victims.
- Look in the phone book under counseling, social work, and psychologists for therapists who advertise that they deal with the issues of abuse.

When choosing a therapist, plan to interview several of those whose names you've gathered before setting up any scheduled counseling sessions. When interviewing them, remember that you have the right to ask questions. An understanding therapist will be willing to give you the answers you need. This list of questions compiled by Betty Holland can help guide you in what to look for. Some of these questions are appropriate to ask the therapist in an interview; others will serve as guidelines in your own assessment of the therapist. You may not be able to answer many of them until you have experienced at least one counseling session with that therapist.

## Questions to Consider as You Choose a Therapist

1. What is his/her method—Inner child, guided imagery, visualization, behavior modification? (Behavior modification alone cannot heal the Inner Child or bring about a change of heart.)

2. What is his/her fee? How long are the sessions?

3. Is he/she healthy (emotionally, physically, spiritually)?

4. Is he/she open and willing to learn?

5. What is his/her attitude toward women or men?

6. How much experience has he/she had with guided imagery?

7. Does he/she study and keep current with recent developments in psychotherapy?

8. Do I feel I can communicate with and trust him/her?

9. Has he/she done his/her own healing and Inner Child work?

10. Is he/she a good listener who believes and validates my experiences?

11. Does he/she help me look at myself honestly, be more self-aware, and discover my personal truth?

12. Does he/she help me discover my own path to healing?

13. Will he/she respect my personal and religious beliefs?

14. What is his/her belief about working with my past?

15. Am I listening to my Inner Child's preference in whether to choose a male or a female therapist?

After interviewing each prospective therapist, take time to assess how you felt with them. Did you feel at ease? Did you trust him or her? Did you feel believed and validated? Once you have gathered sufficient information to make a decision, ask Heavenly Father to confirm your decision. If you don't feel good about this particular therapist, choose another, and ask the questions again. If you do feel it is right, make an appointment. After one appointment with the therapist, reassess your feelings and see how many more of the checklist questions you feel you can answer. You are totally free to change therapists at any point.

You may find a therapist you can work with well throughout your entire recovery. Or you may choose one, see him or her for a while, then decide you need someone else. Remember, it is okay to change therapists! If your psychological, physical, or spiritual boundaries are violated, leave. It is okay to express your honest feelings about what is going on in your therapy sessions. If you do not like something, tell your therapist. If he or she does not respond to your needs, find one who will.

In my recovery I worked with two different therapists. I went to a female therapist for a while, then felt impressed to change to a male therapist. Each one helped me in a different way by guiding me through the different stages of my healing process. I believe I was led to each one as a result of praying for guidance in choosing professional counseling.

## Finding and Choosing a Support Group

One of the best places I found to share my pain and anger was in a confidential support group. Sharing in a safe, non-judgmental setting with others who believed and validated me helped bring me out of isolation. I knew that coming out of isolation was critical to my healing. Listening to other survivors' thoughts and feelings, and knowing that others had survived experiences as devastating as mine, gave me the strength and hope to keep going.

> *If you are isolated, you must begin to reach out beyond yourself. You simply cannot do this alone. Alone is what you have known your whole life. Alone doesn't work anymore. Alone will perpetuate abuse. Alone you will get sicker and weaker. Alone is death or insanity. Together you can open doors. Together you can trust. Together you can need, feel, and risk. Together you can change and grow. Together you can heal.*
>
> *—A Survivor[1]*

Having the opportunity to meet weekly in a support group with other women of my faith was one of the greatest assets of my recovery. Identifying with other women who had such similar feelings and challenges in their lives was a powerful help for me. It helped me to accept what my dragons were and what I had to do to slay them. I committed myself to go to my support group every week because it kept me in touch with myself and offered me a constant source of support. Witnessing the healing work others were doing also helped me to continue with mine.

## Types of Groups

There are many different types of support groups you may wish to consider as an aid in your recovery experience. The following is a list of the most common types with a brief description of each:

**1. Self-Help Support Groups.** A support group offers you the opportunity to "mourn with those who mourn" (Mosiah 18:8-9), and "bear . . . one another's burdens" (Galatians 6:2). This type of group is free of charge, has been organized by lay people who control all functions, but it is not a quick-fix program. Most groups of this type consist of people who have a similar purpose—to overcome their pain and problems. They have come together to share their life stories confidentially and to receive support from one another.

Such group meetings are either guided by an appointed chairperson or participants rotate as group leader. Most communities have support groups that meet weekly. Local hospitals and therapists usually have a list of the different meeting times of local groups. In some areas where the LDS Church is prominent, support groups have been organized by local priesthood leaders with the help of a designated social services representative or a recovered survivor. If these resources are not available in your area, perhaps you can be instrumental in starting a group.

You can counsel with local church leaders to learn how to start a support group for survivors who are of your faith. You may experience important benefits from meeting with a support group comprised of other survivors who are of your own faith instead of with a community group. Community groups may restrict the opportunity to speak freely about God and Jesus Christ. Most of these groups do acknowledge the need to turn to a "Higher Power" in recovery, but participants are not free to speak openly and specifically about their beliefs, or to use scriptures, or to offer prayers.

The support group I attended was organized specifically for LDS women. We opened each meeting with prayer and invited the Holy Ghost to be present. The designated chairperson then shared a gospel message from the scriptures or another source, to offer strength and hope and to encourage personal growth. Following the chairperson's message, the meeting was open to anyone who wanted to share. We closed the meeting by kneeling in prayer to give thanks for the Spirit that we felt had guided us and for the opportunity to heal in a safe setting.

Attending this support group offered me a profound healing experience. To speak openly and honestly about my pain in a confidential setting with other LDS women, where we turned to the scriptures for answers and called upon our Heavenly Father to lead us in our healing and asked for the Holy Ghost to guide us, was one of the most powerful experiences of my recovery. (For format guidelines in holding a support group for survivors, see the Appendix.)

**2. Twelve-Step Groups.** A twelve-step group is the same as a self-help/support group but is based on twelve steps or beliefs that are shared at the beginning of each meeting. These twelve steps offer the participant a guide to healing as they are applied during the recovery experience. Alcoholics Anonymous is the "granddaddy" of twelve-step groups. In the fifty years since the beginning of Alcoholics Anonymous, many other groups have been founded using the twelve-step format.

There is a twelve-step group for just about every behavioral problem that exists. Specific twelve-step groups may be helpful if you are trying to overcome addictions. Overeaters Anonymous exists for eating addictions, Alcoholics Anonymous for alcoholism, Co-dependents Anonymous (CODA) for relationship problems, etc. Local chapter numbers for groups are usually listed in the phone book or can be found by calling local hospitals. These groups are nondenominational but all of them refer to a "Higher Power" in their twelve beliefs, teaching the essential truth that one must turn things over to a "Higher Power" in order to fully recover.

Twelve-step groups have helped millions of addicted people throughout the world and, because they are spiritually based, can help survivors even when the group limits the sharing of gospel beliefs.

**3. Therapy Groups.** These groups are interactive; group members share and work on their issues with the help of the therapist and other group participants. They frequently offer exercises such as role-playing and visualization work. Having a therapist present in a group experience can help members who need guidance in their recovery. A therapist can also make sure no one gets out of control.

These groups are run by professional therapists and usually cost money. They generally run for a given period of time such as eight or twelve weeks, with meetings once a week. In order to participate well in this kind of support group, you must feel comfortable sharing in the presence of an authority figure and be comfortable receiving advice in the group setting.

You must be very careful when choosing a support group. Be wary of programs that offer "quick-fixes"— weekend retreats that claim to offer fast remedies for your emotional problems. Do not allow yourself to stay in situations that challenge your beliefs and values. Again, pray to know what kind of support group you should get involved with, and to know when it is time to quit or change groups. You will be guided in your quest.

## What to Look for in a Self-Help Support Group

Here are some questions to ask yourself when deciding whether the support group you are considering is a safe and helpful setting for some of your recovery work:

1. Trust: Does the group offer an atmosphere in which I can build trust with myself and others? Does it offer a base of unconditional love and support?
2. Affirmations: Do I receive consistent messages affirming that I am okay just as I am?
3. Confidentiality: Do I feel safe to talk about my feelings—such as shame, pain, and anger? (What is said in a support group meeting must stay there. No one is to share anyone's story or grief at any time with anyone outside the support group.)
4. No Cross-Talk: Do I feel believed and validated? (No one contradicts or interrupts another person while he or she is sharing.)
5. Personal Boundaries: Am I free to share my religious beliefs and values? Is sharing these beliefs in a group setting important to me? Are my personal boundaries respected and not violated? (Each person in the group is responsible for understanding and setting their own physical, emotional, and spiritual boundaries.)
6. Group Guidelines: Does the group have boundaries that have been established for the benefit of the entire group? (Group members should feel that is okay to leave at any time, especially if they feel unsafe and uncomfortable. They should also be allowed to remain silent when they don't feel like sharing; they can just be there.)

1. *In Reflection,* monthly newsletter, (Portland, Oregon: December 1991), Vol. 1, No. 9, p. 5.

# CHAPTER 6
## SETTING HEALTHY BOUNDARIES

*1) I walk down the street*
*There is a deep hole in the sidewalk.*
*I fall in.*
*I am lost...I am hopeless.*
*It isn't my fault.*
*It takes forever to find a way out*

*2) I walk down the same street.*
*There is a deep hole in the sidewalk.*
*I pretend I don't see it.*
*I fall in again.*
*I can't believe I am in the same place.*
*But, it isn't my fault.*
*It still takes a long time to get out.*

*3) I walk down the same street*
*There is a deep hole in the sidewalk.*
*I see it is there.*
*I still fall in...it's a habit.*
*My eyes are open.*
*I know where I am.*
*It is my fault.*
*I get out immediately.*

*4) I walk down the same street.*
*There is a deep hole in the sidewalk.*
*I walk around it.*

*5) I walk down another street.*
— *Portia Nelson[1]*

*W*hen I was abused, my boundaries, my right to say no, my sense of power in the world, were violated. I was not given a chance to learn how to set boundaries because I was powerless to do so.

Boundaries help us develop a sense of empowerment in our lives. Empowerment to me is the opposite of powerlessness and helplessness. As victims we learned to feel powerless and helpless. As a survivor you will learn to set boundaries and to become self-empowered.

Empowerment is knowing and feeling my right to make choices, to act on those choices, and to respond to the consequences of my choices. Empowerment is knowing who I am, owning myself, standing up for myself, and taking responsibility for my life. Learning about boundaries and how to set and reinforce them was essential to my recovery.

## What is a Boundary?

Boundaries are limits that help give our lives structure and form. John Bradshaw teaches us that one of our basic needs is structure. We ensure our structure by developing a boundary system within which we safely operate. Structure gives our lives form. Boundaries offer us safety and allow a more efficient use of energy. [2]

Boundaries offer us protection from the damaging words and actions of others and our own self-defeating behaviors. Boundaries help us to establish limits and guidelines that are necessary in order to recover. The following are some examples of what boundaries mean to me and other survivors I know:

- A boundary is knowing where you stop and where I begin.
- A boundary is being able to say "No!"
- A boundary is knowing I have choices.
- A boundary is for my safety.
- Boundaries allow me to make my own choices.
- Boundaries allow me to heal.
- Boundaries allow me to grow.
- Boundaries allow me to think clearly.
- Boundaries protect me from spinning out of control.
- With boundaries, my life becomes clearer.
- When I have no boundaries people walk all over me.
- Boundaries help me to establish positive self-worth and self-esteem. I have more self-respect when I have boundaries. When I treat myself with self-respect, others do too.
- Boundaries allow me to protect my spirit.

Each of us needs internal and external boundaries. Internal boundaries have to do with our own behavior and thought patterns. They offer us limits and guidelines for our emotional, behavioral, and spiritual growth. External boundaries have to do with other people and events. They allow us to have a set of rules to govern how we will allow others to treat us, and rules that protect us from dangerous and defeating experiences.

It is especially important to establish boundaries in relationships because boundaries allow us to love ourselves and others more purely. Jesus taught us that the perfect law of love is to "love one another as I have loved you" (John 15:12). How has Jesus loved us? He loves us with an unconditional love. The scriptures teach us that this pure love of Christ is called charity. We learn that without charity, without the capacity to offer Christlike love to others, we are nothing.

> Wherefore, my beloved . . ., if ye have not charity, ye are nothing, for charity never faileth. Wherefore, cleave unto charity, which is the greatest of all, for all things must fail—
> But charity is the pure love of Christ, and it endureth forever; and whoso is found possessed of it at the last day, it shall be well with [her]. (Moroni 7:46-47.)

In order to really love, to have charity, you first need to have a sense of yourself. In order to have a sense of yourself, you need boundaries. Aileen Clyde of the General Relief Society Presidency of the LDS Church, teaches us that even the experience of charity needs boundaries, that as we learn to have charity, we must also learn to set boundaries in order to protect ourselves.

> It is not charity or kindness to endure any type of abuse or unrighteousness that may be inflicted on us by others. God's commandment that as we love him, we must respect ourselves, suggests we must not accept disrespect from others. It is not charity to let another repeatedly deny our divine nature and agency. It is not charity to bow down in despair and helplessness. That kind of suffering should be ended.[3]

Setting healthy internal and external boundaries will help enable you to stop any kind of abuse you may still be experiencing. Here are some examples of internal and external boundaries:

## Internal Boundaries

- I will set boundaries.
- I will make time to do the work of recovery.
- I will not beat myself up internally for making a mistake; instead, I will see a mistake as a learning experience.
- I can feel and talk about how I feel.
- I will not absorb other people's feelings.
- I can say no and not feel guilty.
- I will learn to trust my Heavenly Father.
- I will learn to pray every day.
- I will celebrate my successes.
- I don't have to be perfect.
- I don't have to be the best in everything I do.
- I will not compare myself to other people.
- I can be who I am because that is good enough.
- I will receive and believe in my heart the honest compliments and affirmations of others.
- I can be open, honest, and direct when I communicate.
- I will learn to appropriately experience and manage my anger.
- I can enjoy life without feeling guilty.
- I will admit I am powerless to my addictions and get help.
- I will not project blame for my problems on other people.
- I will take responsibility for stopping my self-defeating behaviors and for seeking worthwhile support that will help me stop them.

## External Boundaries

- I have the right to heal and to do the work of healing, regardless of the opinion of friends, or how family members respond to me.
- I now choose to associate with people who treat me with respect and kindness.
- I will not associate with people who are cruel and

unsupportive. I realize that no one can make me feel inferior unless I give them permission.

- I will not put other people's feelings before my own.
- I will consider their feelings after I understand how I am feeling.
- I am not responsible for taking care of other people's feelings.
- I will not tell other people what to do with their lives.
- I will learn to listen and offer support by validating other people.
- I will not allow other people to tell me what to do with my life.
- I will learn to share my abuse only with safe people in safe places.
- I will not subject myself to people and events that make me feel uneasy and powerless.
- During the work of my healing, I can limit or avoid altogether contact with people who trigger my unresolved issues, which causes my healing to regress.
- I can allow people back into my life when I feel I am ready to have a relationship with them (this includes family members).
- I can decide what boundaries I need in my relationships. If others do not honor my boundaries, I can choose to stop the relationship.
- I can limit my sexual relations during the work of my healing. When I heal, I can choose to have sexual relations (within the bounds I have set) when I want to give and receive sexually.
- I want to express my sexuality within the bounds God has set.
- I will protect myself from the emotional, spiritual, physical, and sexual abuse of others. I have a right to stop it.
- I will also learn to recognize my own abusive behaviors and learn to stop them.

Each of us must learn what boundaries we need to set, set them, and then be responsible for maintaining them. No one else knows exactly what we need, and no one else should be expected to take care of us by setting boundaries for us. Several years ago, I came across a picture of myself standing in the garage vacuuming out some storage units. The picture shows me seven months pregnant with a cast on my broken arm. And because I suffer from severe hayfever, I had a large bandanna tied around my face since it was the height of allergy season. I looked at that photo that my husband had snapped and asked myself, "What in the world am I doing working in the garage in that condition?" I turned to my husband and said, "If I were in a wheelchair and there was work to be done in the garage, I'd tell you to roll me on out." He quickly responded, "And I would!" Fifty light bulbs suddenly went on in my head letting me know—"Carol, you are responsible for taking care of you. Nobody else will, so don't expect them to. And guess what, you're the best one to do it anyway!" Each of us has the power within us to learn what we need and to do what needs to be done.

Studying the scriptures gives us insight into the guidelines and limits the Lord has set for us. God has eternal boundaries. They are guidelines and limits that give us power. Learning about and living according to God's boundaries gives us the ability to know what boundaries we need.

> Abide in me, and I in you. As the branch cannot bear fruit of itself, except it abide in the vine; no more can ye, except ye abide in me.
> I am the vine, ye are the branches; [She] that abideth in me, and I in [her], the same bringeth forth much fruit: for without me ye can do nothing. (John 15:4-5.)

## How Do I Set and Maintain My Boundaries?

When I started to set boundaries during my recovery, it was a very scary and painful experience. It scared me because I thought other people would hate me. I believed that if I didn't give people what they wanted, I would be abandoned again. As I learned that the abuse was not my fault and that I did not have to give people what they wanted, I realized that I had the right to take care of myself regardless of others' reactions.

I was frightened but I set boundaries anyway! I knew that I needed boundaries to continue to progress in my healing. I set both internal and external boundaries that helped protect me from regressing back into the painful feelings of victimization. I learned that most of the people I wanted a relationship with honored my boundaries. I separated myself from people who were not emotionally safe for me during my recovery, and as a result I was free from their negative and damaging reactions. As my recovery progressed my boundaries changed. I learned that boundaries need not be set in concrete. I could set them, test them, evaluate them, and change them as needed.

As you heal and grow, you too will learn to be flexible and change your boundaries to fit your needs. Your feelings will help you determine what boundaries you need to set. Listen to feelings like pain, fear, anger, frustration, abandonment, confusion, then ask yourself these questions: Why am I feeling this way? What boundaries do I need to set in order to feel better about my life and myself?

Start small. Set one boundary, practice it, then set another. Keep in mind that, although you're working on the present, situations will come along on a regular basis that need new boundaries.

When you set an internal boundary, you may find it helps to write it down. I wrote down each boundary fifteen to twenty times to help it sink in. Then I checked myself daily, to see how well I had honored my boundary. I developed a system to help me improve gradually without beating myself up along the way for making mistakes. For example, I honored the boundary of not dumping my anger on my children by choosing to manage my anger in a healthy way and choosing not to yell or rage at them.

When you are in recovery, it is very hard to have full control of your emotions at all times. Setting the boundary of not yelling at your children all week is admirable but can result in more feelings of failure when you aren't able to honor the boundary all the time. In order to experience success in honoring a boundary, you need to determine where you are and where you want to be. First, decide how you are doing on a scale of one to ten, with one being the worst and ten being the ideal.

Let's say you decide you are at two and you would like to be at four. Ideally you may like to be at nine or ten, but in order to get there you need to start small. Allow yourself to experience success daily by keeping a record of your progress. This is easily done by marking on a chart (you can create your own). Rate yourself daily, using measures like the scale of one to ten, or yes/no.

I preferred scales because they allowed more room for error and allowed me to experience success while I was still making mistakes. For example, let's say I honored a boundary of not yelling at my children three out of five times one day; I chose to manage my emotions in a healthier way. So I rated myself with a five because I honored my boundary with partial success. I did better! This method worked for setting and maintaining all kinds of boundaries, and helped me progress a day at a time. With the success of setting and honoring new boundaries in my life, I learned to celebrate my growth. I didn't expect to be able to honor any boundary perfectly. If I had simply improved, I would congratulate myself and do something nice for myself. This helped reinforce the belief that I was a person of worth who deserved to have good things happen.

When I set a boundary that involved other people, I often had to figure out beforehand what I was going to say to them. I would write it down, then practice it. I called these my boundary scripts. They were especially helpful when I was talking on the phone with the person I was sharing my boundary with because I could read my words and stay focused. I wrote this script to help me say no politely: "Thank you for asking me, but I'm not free to do that at this time." I didn't need to say why or apologize. It seemed to work well and still does when I have reached my boundary of how much I can do for others outside the home.

As you begin to set boundaries, people may not believe you are serious and may not support your boundaries at first. As Harriet Goldhor Lerner teaches in her book, *The Dance of Anger*, other people commonly meet our actions with a countermove or *change back* reaction whenever we give up old styles of behavior. This is especially true for family members who are used to your acting and reacting in a certain way. If you do not initially receive support for your boundary, ask them again to honor your boundary. Explain that in order for you to work toward a good relationship, you need your boundary to be honored. A survivor shares the following example:

> *My husband was in the habit of putting me down with sarcastic and negative comments. They were always cloaked in humor and I had allowed myself to accept them through the years. As part of my recovery I realized that these comments were very painful and shaming to me. I decided to set a boundary with him and asked him to please not put me down anymore because it was very painful to*

*me. I told him that I was a worthwhile person and would like to have communication that was free from disrespect and sarcastic humor.*

*He must have thought I wasn't serious because he continued to put me down, with the excuse that "he was only kidding, couldn't I take a joke?" After allowing the putdowns to happen several more times, I decided to state this boundary every time he did it: "You just put me down, and I don't want you to do that anymore. If you want to have a good relationship with me, you will support my boundaries." After I shared this with him several times, he stopped his putdowns.*

*—A Survivor*

Ultimately the hope is that other people will grow and change along with us, strengthening emotional ties in our relationships as we grow and change. However, this does not always occur because we cannot control other people's reactions to us. We each live in an environment where our choices affect other people's lives. It is important to be aware of how our boundaries effect other people and be prepared for other people's efforts to change us back to who they think we should be.

As your recovery progresses, you will get a feel for which boundaries you can let go of and which ones you still need. You will be able to set new boundaries as you experience new opportunities and relationships. You can know what boundaries you need through the power of the Holy Ghost, as you ask to know through prayer. You will find that as you set and maintain your boundaries, you will feel less fear and powerlessness and develop the attributes that are mentioned in 2 Timothy 1:7, "For God has not given us the spirit of fear; but of power, and of love, and of a sound mind."

Power, love, and a sound mind are the gifts we receive when we set healthy boundaries. As a result of having boundaries, you will begin to act with confidence. You will know that you are a person of worth and value—a person who deserves good things in her life. The following story illustrates how setting boundaries changed the life of one survivor:

> *I have always been what is now referred to as a "co-dependent" person. I have very willingly taken the blame for many things that were never my fault. "Peace at any price" has been an unspoken law in my life. If anyone was unhappy, I found myself apologizing, and trying to "fix" everything. When I was treated rudely, or if I felt my feelings were not considered, I would just smile and say, "Don't worry about it. It's not that big of a deal." I found it just about impossible to speak out when I felt uncomfortable. Even if I was in a truly compromising situation, somehow it seemed that I didn't have the right to say how I felt.*
>
> *I have come to understand that my lack of boundaries, and the feeling that I was not a person of value, were two reasons why I have not been able to protect myself. I am learning that I am a person of great value, that I deserve to be treated with respect, and that I have the right to speak out when I have been disregarded or violated.*
>
> *As I have become stronger and my value as a child of God has become clearer, my personal relationships have changed dramatically. I will not allow myself to be abused any longer. My thoughts and feelings are just as important as those of others in the relationship. I have a right to say "Please don't use my things without asking," or "I feel hurt when you say*

*or do that to me." To some this may seem very basic, but it represents over a year of hard work to get to this place in my life.*

*I am learning to be more confident and assertive on the job. In the past I was told by my co-workers that I didn't have much self-confidence, and I know that some people doubted my ability to perform my daily tasks. As I grow stronger, I feel more confident, and I know that I give that feeling to others, too. I feel less anxiety when I have to make decisions, or to perform tasks in a precise way. My confidence is growing every day. I am a much happier person. I know I am moving in the right direction, one step at a time.*

*—A Survivor[4]*

This survivor expresses clearly the key ingredient for successful growth: "moving in the right direction, one step at a time."

Learning to take care of ourselves by setting healthy boundaries is hard work. In Hebrews 12:1 we are counseled to "run with patience the race that is set before us." Running is hard work; it takes a lot of strength, a lot of endurance. Continually improving your capacity to set and maintain boundaries is hard work. It also takes strength and endurance.

The race that is set before you is your recovery. The interesting thing about this race is that you are the only one in it and there is no time to beat. It is your race to be run with patience. And just like good runners know how to protect themselves from injury and fatigue during the race, you too can learn to protect yourself. You can protect yourself from the harmful comments and actions of others and from your own self-defeating behaviors by setting and maintaining healthy boundaries during your recovery and for the rest of your life.

1. Portia Nelson, "Autobiography in Five Short Chapters," *There's a Hole in My Sidewalk.* New York: Popular Library, 1977.
2. John Bradshaw, *Healing the Shame that Binds You.* Deerfield Beach, Florida: Health Communications, Inc., 1988, p.4.
3. "Charity Suffereth Long," *Ensign*, November 1991, p. 77.
4. *In Reflection*, monthly newsletter, (Portland, Oregon: March 1991), Vol.1, No. 12, p. 2.

# PART TWO
# THE SPIRITUAL PATH TO HEALING

# CHAPTER 7
## SPIRITUAL GRIEF

*I waited patiently for the Lord; and he inclined unto me, and heard my cry.*

*He brought me up also out of an horrible pit, out of the miry clay, and set my feet upon a rock, and established my goings.*

*And he hath put a new song in my mouth, even praise unto our God: many shall see it, and fear, and shall trust in the Lord. (Psalms 40:1-3.)*

I have found that the survivor of child sexual abuse and incest suffers not only profound emotional losses but also profound spiritual losses. These losses constitute spiritual abuse. Spiritual losses and damage to the spirit must also be grieved. I was not able to heal completely until I mourned my spiritual losses. Incest and child sexual abuse is "soul murder" because of the damage it does to the guileless spirit of the Inner Child.

As a survivor of child sexual abuse, my spiritual development was greatly impaired. Grieving my spiritual losses led me to an understanding of why I was abused and to freedom from feelings of anger, abandonment, and betrayal toward God. It also helped me to discover what I could learn from my spiritual abuse. I'm so grateful that I turned to my Lord and Savior, Jesus Christ; I learned to trust and obey him and to submit myself to him. In return for my obedience, he offered me the blessings of healing that were available to me through the atonement.

## "Why Me?"

As survivors of incest and child sexual abuse, most of us at one time or another, ask these questions or some variation of them: "Why did it happen to me? What's wrong with me? What's wrong with my family? Why didn't my family stop it? Why didn't I stop it? Why didn't God stop it?"

As you ask and answer any of these "why" questions, please know that you are not responsible for the abuse—you did nothing to cause it. You probably have lived most of your life blaming yourself or God for the tragedy and its residual effects, but the answers to the question of "why" have nothing to do with you. It is still important that you probe the "why" of your abuse, however, because this will enable you to relieve your Inner Child from the pain of feeling responsible.

As a child I tried to ask some "why" questions only to receive inadequate, incomplete answers. I have since learned that the answers to the "why" questions can be found in understanding more clearly the laws of individual agency as they relate to the experience of mortality and in learning about the power the survivor has in breaking down the generational sins of the fathers. By answering the "why me?" question, I was able to let go of all self-blame, accept my history, and move further along my path to wholeness.

## Agency and the Experience of Mortality

I believe that we once lived in a premortal existence where we chose to come to an earth that has the provisions of agency and choice. (See Abraham 3:26-28, Moses 4: 1-4,

Revelation 12: 7-9.) The decision to be born was our own. As a result of that decision, we also agreed to come into a life where we would experience love, peace, happiness, joy, and the freedom to choose right or wrong. In order to fully experience and appreciate the richness of these conditions, we knew we would also have to experience pain, suffering, trauma, darkness, and the possible injustice of another's choice to victimize us.

In the Doctrine and Covenants 29:39 the Lord teaches us this principle: "And it must needs be that the devil should tempt the children of men, or they could not be agents unto themselves; for if they never should have bitter they could not know the sweet." (See also D&C 29: 36-39, D&C 93: 29-30.)

Incest and child sexual abuse happens because we chose to come to mortality and take the risk of experiencing the consequences of others' choices—the good with the evil. Your abuse is the result of another person's unrighteous use of agency. Their assault on your personal power and freedom has caused you to suffer painful and crippling spiritual, emotional, and physical residual effects. But it can also be the catalyst of some of the greatest growth and learning you will ever experience in your life.

In her remarks at a Brigham Young University Women's Conference, Francine Bennion teaches us why we agreed to endure suffering in this life: "We suffer because we were willing to pay the cost of being and of being here with others in their ignorance and inexperience as well as our own ignorance and inexperience. We suffer because we are willing to pay the cost of living with laws of nature, which operate quite consistently whether or not we understand them or can manage them."[1]

I realized that my personal righteousness had nothing to do with the abuse I suffered as a child. It was not my choice, but someone else's. My belief in the gospel did not protect me from the evils of the world or the agency of unrighteous individuals. However, the gospel does provide me with the guidance and spiritual tools that I need to overcome the negative effects of anything I encounter in this mortal experience.

We are promised in Alma 36:3 "that whosoever shall put their trust in God shall be supported in their trials, and their troubles, and their afflictions, and shall be lifted up at the last day." Isaiah has taught us that if we live the gospel and obey our covenants, Christ will give "power to the faint; and to them that have no might he increaseth strength." Those who "wait upon the Lord shall renew their strength; they shall mount up with wings as eagles; they shall run, and not be weary; and they shall walk, and not faint" (Isaiah 40:29, 31). (See also Alma 44:4, Helaman 5:12.)

Marriage and family therapist Carlfred Broderick bears personal witness of these truths: "The gospel of Jesus Christ is not insurance against pain. It is resource in event of pain, and when that pain comes (and it will come because we came here on earth to have pain among other things), when it comes, rejoice that you have resource to deal with your pain."[2]

In the Book of Mormon, Jacob, the son of Lehi and younger brother of Nephi, "suffered afflictions and much sorrow" in his childhood "because of the rudeness of [his] brethren." As a result of this suffering he turned to the Lord and came to know "the greatness of God." In a blessing administered by his father, God promised Jacob that He would "consecrate thine afflictions for thy good" (2 Nephi 2:1-2).

Webster defines the word consecrate this way: "to set apart as holy; devote to sacred or serious use." Jacob prepared himself for receiving that consecration by coming to know the Lord and His greatness. After he developed this faith he called upon God for His help and then lived a life worthy to receive it. We too have the gospel tools to allow our afflictions to be consecrated for our good. We must follow the same steps as Jacob did by having faith in Christ's power and asking for it through prayer.

## Generational Sins and Dysfunction

Sexual abuse is often a multi-generational problem cloaked in a vicious cycle of secrecy. Incest and the sexual abuse of children can go on in a family for generations without the cycle being broken. The cycle of sexual abuse and incest is difficult to break due to the shame associated with it and the need to keep it secret and hidden. Victims become perpetrators or wounded adults who may not even remember their abuse. Many survivors are afraid to share the reality of their abuse because of deep-seated feelings of shame and the fear of not being believed.

## Saviors on Mount Zion

If you are a survivor of incest or parental child abuse, most likely the person who molested you was also a victim, who was molested by another victim, who was molested by another victim, and on and on back through the generations. This domino effect has caused you to become temporarily "lost, because of the transgression of [your] parents" (2 Nephi 2:21). But you have chosen a different path by your decision to heal. You are unwilling to pass this suffering on to another generation. You have become a "transition person" or in Carlfred Broderick's words, a "Savior on Mount Zion":

> Indeed, my experience in various church callings and in my profession as a family therapist has convinced me that God actively intervenes in some destructive lineages, assigning a valiant spirit

to break the chain of destructiveness in such families. Although these children may suffer innocently as victims of violence, neglect, and exploitation, through the grace of God some find the strength to 'metabolize' the poison within themselves, refusing to pass it on to future generations. Before them were generations of destructive pain; after them the line flows clear and pure. Their children and children's children will call them blessed.

In suffering innocently that others might not suffer, such persons, in some degree, become as "saviors on Mount Zion" by helping to bring salvation to a lineage.

In a former era, the Lord sent a flood to destroy unworthy lineages. In this generation, it is my faith that he has sent numerous choice individuals to help purify them.[3]

It is my personal belief that in a premortal life you may have agreed to come to your family with the purpose of interrupting the generational sins of your family line. Many of God's children received instruction before coming to this earth. In D&C 138:56 we learn that "even before they were born they, with many others, received their first lessons in the world of spirits and were prepared to come forth in due time of the Lord to labor in his vineyard for the salvation of the souls of men."

As a survivor you are learning healthier ways to take care of yourself and healthier ways to parent. By healing yourself, you are building "the old waste places" to "raise up the foundations of many generations" to be called "The repairer of the breach, The restorer of paths to dwell in" (Isaiah 58:12). We are a "chosen generation" which has been called "out of darkness" to receive Christ's "marvelous light"

(1 Peter 2:9). One survivor has put it in these poignant, compelling words:

> *I am sick of the family sickness that I have seen and experienced. I am tired of seeing the pain I have passed on to my own children. They deserve more, but in order to give them more I have to face the lies and the pain, and get rid of all the junk passed on to me from generations behind me.*
>
> *—A Survivor*

Another survivor said it this way:

> *Satan may have assaulted you through your father. Your father gave you his darkness. Your physical life was the stewardship of your father and mother, you have the stewardship of your spiritual birth with Christ.*
>
> *The Lord needed your strength to precipitate the healing in your whole family. This could not happen if you didn't suffer these trials. You will teach healing of family sexual abuse simply through going through your healing. The Lord did not abandon you, he has been waiting for you to come to him. Accept your trials and don't blame the Lord. He is there for you.*
>
> *—A Survivor*

If you are currently inflicting abuse of any kind on another human being, please seek help and commit yourself to a recovery program. We must all be willing to do as Dennis Rasmussen advises in his book, *The Lord's Question*:

> To hallow my life, [God] taught me to endure sorrow rather than cause it, to restrain anger rather than heed it, to bear injustice rather than

inflict it. 'Resist not evil,' [Jesus] said in the Sermon on the Mount (Matthew 5:39). Evil multiplies by the response it seeks to provoke, and when I return evil for evil, I engender corruption myself. The chain of evil is broken for good when a pure and loving heart absorbs a hurt and forbears to hurt in return.[4]

## The Purposes of Suffering

I do not believe that God inflicts suffering on us. I believe that we are allowed to experience suffering and should use it to grow spiritually and to draw closer to the Lord. Pain and suffering can be our most powerful learning tools if we choose to use them in this way. I believe, as Marian S. Bergin says, "The process of my pain has been the process of my learning."[5]

Anne Morrow Lindbergh, author and wife of the famous pilot Charles Lindbergh, experienced great suffering when her baby was kidnapped and eventually murdered. Reflecting back on this trauma she wrote, "I do not believe that sheer suffering teaches. If suffering alone taught, all the world would be wise, since everyone suffers. To suffering must be added mourning, understanding, patience, love, openness, and the willingness to remain vulnerable." [6] As a survivor of sexual abuse, I found that if I took this perspective, I could allow my suffering to teach me.

## What Can We Learn from the Abuse and Suffering?

Heavenly Father knew we would suffer, so in his wisdom he provided us with a way to learn from our suffering. The experience of recovering from incest and sexual abuse can create a powerful desire to know Christ and the power of his gospel. "Adversity, even when caused willfully by others' unrestrained appetite, can be a source of growth when viewed from the perspective of eternal principle."[7]

"The greatest lessons I've learned from my recovery," says one survivor, "have not been how to recover from incest. The greatest lessons have been to come to know and feel the power of Jesus Christ and his gospel, and the power I have to become whole through him."

There are times I find it difficult to look upon adversity as a gift. I have endured long periods of pain and suffering. As a child I was forced to suffer unjustly, and as an adult it felt like I was again forced to suffer the pain and trauma of my abuse as I went through the recovery process. But I also realized that my current suffering was completing what I did not have the capacity to feel and experience as a child. Healing the wounds of my abuse was a very painful process.

There will be times during your recovery when you will feel as a modern prophet felt: "O God, where art thou? And where is the pavilion that covereth thy hiding place? How long shall thy hand be stayed, and thine eye, yea thy pure eye, behold from the eternal heavens the wrongs of thy people and of thy servants, and thine ear be penetrated with their cries?" (D&C 121:1-2).

You may feel as oppressed as Job in the Old Testament and feel that death would be a blessing to save you from suffering one more day of pain. In his agony Job could see no reason for or end to his suffering.

The Lord has given comfort and counsel to his children in their deepest periods of pain. You may find it helpful to read the Lord's counsel as if these passages were written to you:

> My [daughter], peace be unto thy soul; thine adversity and thine afflictions shall be but a small moment; And then, if thou endure it well, God shall exalt thee on high; thou shalt triumph over all thy foes. (D&C 121:7-8.)

If the heavens gather blackness, and all the elements combine to hedge up the way; and above all, if the very jaws of hell shall gape open the mouth wide after thee, know thou, my [daughter], that all these things shall give thee experience, and shall be for thy good. (D&C 122:7.)

And again, be patient in tribulation until I come; and, behold, I come quickly, and my reward is with me, and they who have sought me early shall find rest to their souls. Even so. Amen. (D&C 54:10.)

For I know that my redeemer liveth, and that he shall stand at the latter day upon the earth:
And though after my skin worms destroy this body, yet in my flesh shall I see God:
Whom I shall see for myself, and mine eyes shall behold, and not another; though my reins be consumed within me. (Job 19: 25-27.)

I have found adversity and suffering can be a source of spiritual growth and development depending on our response to it. In my recovery, I turned to the Lord in prayer and asked him to help me to know how to endure my suffering, and asked that I would be able to learn from it.

I wanted relief from my pain and suffering immediately. However, recovery takes time, and the time it takes is different for different people. You will probably experience bits and pieces of understanding and hope, here and there, over a period of time.

As you walk the path to wholeness, put your faith in Christ for he "maketh thee whole" (Acts 9:34). He will "prove" us (Abraham 3:25), and when our "hearts [are] depressed, and we [are] about to turn back, behold, the Lord comfort[s] us, and [says] . . . bear with patience thine afflictions, and I will give unto you success" (Alma 26:27). We have been promised this: "If ye observe to do whatsoever I command you, I, the Lord, will turn away all wrath and indignation from you, and the gates of hell shall not prevail against you" (D&C 98:22). You will begin to feel as Micah in the Old Testament:

> Therefore I will look unto the Lord; I will wait for the God of my salvation: my God will hear me.
> Rejoice not against me, O mine enemy: when I fall, I shall arise; when I sit in darkness, the Lord shall be a light unto me. (Micah 7:7-8.)

In times of deep and anguishing pain I held fast to this thought:

> Each of us has a pedigree of divinity. We are daughters of a perfect God. That realization alone gives [knowledge of our] worth to each of us. We must continue to build ourselves and love ourselves enough that when challenges face us, we will use these opportunities to grow rather than to fall. Every woman carries within herself the makings of a successful social being. Joy, strength, and our own future are all within us, and not out there someplace. We make the difference.[8]

I have decided that a survivor need not fully understand suffering during the suffering; however, in time, its value in our lives will become clear. Remembering that our challenges offer us lessons that we need in this mortal experience makes them more acceptable.

## Spiritual Anger and Abandonment

Grieving your spiritual losses is especially important when you have been raised in a family of strong religious tradition and the abuse occurred in your home or was carried out by a church member.

I was raised to trust the members of my family and church. This trust was violated, and I felt emotions of anger and abandonment toward God, the Church, and its members. As a result of releasing my feelings of anger, abandonment, and grief, I was able to let go of feelings of enmity between myself and God and experience a deeper feeling of resolution about my abuse. I was then prepared to experience a spiritual revision which allowed me to offer my trust to the Lord and in humility submit myself to him. You can do the same.

## Anger at God

Allowing myself to become angry at God (and I did!) for feelings of abandonment was a natural part of my healing process. I needed to feel and express my deepest feelings to Heavenly Father and allow Christ to heal my pain. I believe Heavenly Father welcomed my expressions of anger. He understood my pain and was a safe haven where I could share my feelings. I believe Heavenly Father preferred I direct my anger at him rather than at my children and loved ones.

If you don't give your anger to God it may direct itself suddenly and uncontrollably at someone else. Anger is such a strong emotion that it will find a way to be released with or without your direction.

I went to my Father in Heaven in prayer and told him how I felt. I expressed my feelings of abandonment and the trauma I was experiencing in my quest to heal my wounded spirit. I told him how angry I was and how much I hurt. I shared my grief, my sorrow, my shame, and my feelings of abandonment and betrayal. I asked him these questions: "Why did it happen to me? What's wrong with me? What's wrong with my family? Why didn't my family stop it? Why didn't I stop it? Why didn't you stop it?" By expressing these emotions, I let the negative emotional energy out that was trapped inside of me. Saying it released it.

If you choose to express these feelings, remember to do it in a private, safe setting. These feelings are tender and should only be shared with God. Sharing them with others can be damaging for you due to the lack of understanding and harsh judgment you may receive from others. One survivor gives us insight:

> *I could only go so far in my healing and then my anger at God came. How can things like this happen to little children? The separation from my body that was being abused was difficult, but the separation from my heart and feeling was even more traumatic. The separation from my mom was painful but the loss of my connection with God was really tough.*
>
> *As a small child, God was the only one I could count on. Later on as I began the process of healing from my abuse, I became angry at God for what I judged as abandoning and betraying me. How would I ever be able to deal with this? The aloneness was almost more than I could bear. I was so afraid and lost. The traditions of my faith didn't help, church didn't help, words and prayer didn't help—I didn't want to be that vulnerable. But vulnerable I was.*
>
> *I felt defiant toward God. "Father God" and "father abuser" felt too close to each other. I refused to pray to "Father God." I rejected him and everything about him. But that didn't fix the spiritual hunger and need for healing.*

*When a friend suggested I get down on my knees, I said, "Forget it, no way!" The rebellious survivor kid in me would not allow it! But my wound of wounds, my soul wound hurt more than ever. My soul, my spirit, was wounded and in deep need of connection. Even with the need so great, I could not bring myself to turn to the "Father God" I had known as a child.*

*On a rainy fall day, I sat out on the ground by the river as it ran fast and hard and I began to cry and cry and cry. "How could You let this happen to me?" I said in desperation. "I can't believe You let this happen."*

*As I cried, the sky was raining. I looked down on a blade of grass, There were drops of water and the healing words came to me from the Earth, "Don't you know I was crying for you? Don't you know I was with you, grieving for you?"*

*I cried there on the riverbank for a very long time. As my tears fell, I felt a shifting happening within me. I could let in some of that love. I could feel the earth loving me, wanting me to let go some and trust again. I felt like Mother Earth was asking me to try to open just a little. I said yes. I needed to be loved so badly. I was so alone and hurt and scared. I needed to let someone in.*

*God had actually saved me as a child. He knew my secret and I believe today that he saved my life as a small one. I needed to move through the anger and reject the God whom I felt had abandoned me because he was not the real God. Moving through that anger and rejection allowed me to eventually open myself to a more loving compassionate Creator, the true God who loves little children who have been violated. I needed to open to a gentle, powerful*

*protector God. I needed to open, and I did.*
*I realize now that I had rejected God. God had*
*not rejected me!*

*—A Survivor*[9]

It is when you don't seek God's help in resolving this anger that you can become stuck. We are taught that "anger resteth in the bosom of fools" (Ecclesiastes 7:9). Do not let your anger rest within you. Take it to Heavenly Father in prayer and ask Christ to help you resolve it. He will give you the answers and the peace which will lift you closer to him.

## Feeling Forsaken by Your Church and Its Members

In my recovery I also experienced feelings of abandonment and betrayal from my church and its members. These feelings came from wanting and needing them to help parent me in my recovery. I was raised to trust the system of my church and its members; they were supposed to be there for me when I needed help.

In order to let go of these feelings of abandonment and move past them I needed to understand that I was dealing with fallible human beings who were taught not to talk about sexual abuse; most had not learned how to support a survivor. My Inner Child had the false hope that I would be rescued and supported by my church and its members. I realized that I was expecting them to do what only Christ could do for me. "Blessed is the man that trusteth in the Lord, and whose hope the Lord is. Cursed be the man that trusteth in man, and maketh flesh his arm, and whose heart departeth from the Lord" (Jeremiah 17: 7, 5; see also 2 Nephi 4:34).

You, too, are in need of a specific kind of support that is probably not available in traditional church settings. Don't blame others for not giving you what you need if they cannot do so. Through prayer and inspiration you will be led to people who *will* help and support you. Remember that most people are doing the best they know how!

Let go of your feelings of abandonment. Take your wounded Inner Child to Christ. Ask Christ to help you understand those who would not or could not support you in your healing.

Then turn to the physical support that is there for you— a support group, your therapist, a safe friend, or possibly even some family members. Do not focus on who has *not* been there for you, focus on who is there for you now. If you don't have support yet, get it! There are many resources for supporting survivors of incest and child sexual abuse. (See Chapter 5 and the Recovery Resources in Appendix.) Most importantly, continue to keep in touch with your greatest allies—Heavenly Father and Jesus Christ.

In the process of confronting your feelings about your church and its members, one of your deepest resentments may be directed toward male leadership. If you were abused by an active male member who held a priesthood office, you could be dealing with deep feelings of betrayal and blame toward the priesthood and priesthood holders. My solution was to separate them, so that I saw them as two separate entities.

If your abuser served in priesthood offices, rest assured that he did not have the "power of God" just because he served in a calling for the Church. He had to be worthy of this power, which, if he was abusing you, he was not. Elder H. Burke Peterson, explains this in an *Ensign* article addressing unrighteous dominion:

> Some Brethren do not understand that there is
> a marked difference between priesthood authority
> and priesthood power. The two terms are not

necessarily synonymous. Authority in the priesthood comes by laying on of hands by one having
the proper authority. However, according to revelation from the Lord, power in the priesthood
comes only through righteous living.[10]

The Lord teaches us that—

> The rights of the priesthood are inseparably
> connected with the powers of heaven, and that
> the powers of heaven cannot be controlled nor
> handled only upon the principles of righteous-
> ness.
>
> That they may be conferred upon us, it is true;
> but when we undertake to cover our sins, or to
> gratify our pride, our vain ambition, or to exer-
> cise control or dominion or compulsion upon the
> souls of the children of men, in any degree of
> unrighteousness, behold, the heavens withdraw
> themselves; the Spirit of the Lord is grieved; and
> when it is withdrawn, Amen to the priesthood or
> the authority of that man. (D&C 121:36-37.)

A survivor of incest who was molested by her father, a
man who acted in many priesthood offices, came to the
following understanding of her "priesthood wounds" and
how to heal them:

> *A child cannot sin, but the child can receive the
> sins of the parents before baptism. This is sad,
> because those sins of the parents are not removed in
> baptism because they are not the child's sins. The
> child carries these sins through baptism into adult
> life until the adult of that child parents her wounded
> Inner Child and helps her give these burdens to Christ.*

*If the (priesthood holder) perpetrator baptizes his (victim) child she then becomes oppressed with the words from the priesthood in baptism, because spiritually she yearns for the darkness of the abuse to leave at baptism. The child perceives in reality that it is her sin, her badness that is causing the darkness. But in reality the darkness of the abuse is caused by the generational sins passed onto her through her perpetrator.*

*The belief taught to the (victim) child that all her sins will be removed at baptism becomes a lie; it oppresses her because she feels like her sins have not been removed. This is confusing to a (victim) child, especially a child who is baptized by a (priesthood holder) perpetrator. She believes she is left in darkness and despair by the hands of the priesthood. In reality she is left in darkness and despair by her perpetrator, not the priesthood.*

*The survivor lives her life in fear of being shamed by priesthood holders because of the power the (priesthood holder) perpetrator had over her at the time of her victimization.*

*The survivor's responsibility is to take care of this inner darkness and despair by allowing a spiritual rebirth in Christ. It is at that time the darkness and despair of the generational sins will be lifted.*

*—A Survivor*

By making peace with the Church, its members, and the male leadership, you will be letting go of unnecessary inner conflict. This emotional energy can then be directed in more positive ways that will allow you to live in the present. Another benefit of coming to peace with these issues is the ability you will have to separate the Church culture from the gospel. The Church is a means to an end; that end is knowing and living the gospel of Jesus Christ. At this stage of your recovery you will be prepared to experience a spiritual renewal and you will come to understand how the gospel of Jesus Christ can heal your life and how you can be a support to other Church members.

## Spiritual Renewal

Working through my spiritual grief led me to a spiritual awakening—and the development of a genuine, personal relationship with God and Christ. In order to come to this I had to let go of any mental images that painted God as punitive and full of wrath.

By coming to see and experience God as loving, kind, trustworthy, and infallible, I was able to turn to Christ with genuine love and trust. I submitted myself to him. Only by doing this would I be fully able to qualify for the blessings and power available to me through Christ's infinite atonement.

## From Punitive God to Loving God

As a survivor I had to struggle with the effects of someone exercising unrighteous power over me. A residual effect of my abuse was that I conceptualized God as punitive, wrathful, and controlling. Learning to trust God when I found powerful male figures threatening was difficult.

If your abuser was your father or a father-like figure, your image of God has probably been warped by the only thing you knew as a child—a dangerous male authoritative figure.

We are taught in the Old Testament to "fear God." Fearing God does not mean we should see him as the "cop in the sky," rather we should experience awe and reverence for him.

We formulated our perception of God as children. The more frightened and traumatized we were as children, the more spiritual trauma we are likely to feel as survivors. You may feel you somehow deserve God's wrath and punishment and your abuse is a result of that. Relieving your frightened Inner Child of this lie will allow you as an adult to begin to let go of the fear of your earthly father, or father-like abuser, and begin to trust Christ. You deserve Christ's friendship and God's love. By making this transition to a positive image of God, you will begin to experience a deep and loving relationship with him and his son, Jesus Christ.

## Trusting and Submitting

In the scriptures we are taught many, many times to put our trust in God. We are also taught repeatedly that if we trust and submit to Christ we will be assisted in our trials: "The Lord did strengthen them that they could bear up their burdens with ease, and they did submit cheerfully and with patience to all the will of the Lord" (Mosiah 24:15).

Trust means a "complete assurance and certitude regarding the character, ability, strength, or truth of someone." [11] Trusting someone means you can put your hope in them and rely on them. As a child, my abuse taught me not to trust others. During my healing process, I needed to learn not only to trust, but to also submit myself to Heavenly Father and Christ—male authority figures. Submitting meant pain, injustice, and powerlessness to me. Trusting and submitting to someone else, especially a male, was very scary.

My first task in developing trust in Christ was to begin to trust and love myself. I needed to allow myself to feel innately lovable and capable and to believe that Christ cared deeply about me. My next task was to plant the seed of trust in Christ and believe that I could turn to him and that he would be there for me. Numerous scriptures attest to this promise, among them the following:

Put your trust in that Spirit which leadeth to do good—yea, to do justly, to walk humbly, to judge righteously; and this is my spirit.

Verily, verily, I say unto you, I will impart unto you of my Spirit which shall enlighten your mind, which shall fill your soul with joy. (D&C 11:12-13.)

The Lord redeemeth the soul of his servants: and none of them that trust in him shall be desolate. (Psalms 34:22.)

The fear of man bringeth a snare: but whoso putteth his trust in the Lord shall be safe. (Proverbs 29:25.)

But if ye will turn to the Lord with full purpose of heart, and put your trust in him, and serve him with all diligence of mind, if ye do this, he will, according to his own will and pleasure, deliver you out of bondage. (Mosiah 7:33.)

Whosoever shall put their trust in God shall be supported in their trials, and their troubles, and their afflictions, and shall be lifted up at the last day. (Alma 36:3.)

Once you begin to feel genuine trust for Jesus Christ, you can begin to work on learning to submit to him. You must let go of the narrow, negative definition of submission you justly held as a victim and experience submission in a new light. For me personally, offering my will, then yielding to a perfect being, Jesus Christ, was not an act of powerlessness but became, instead, my greatest source of strength.

In your recovery you are working very hard at regaining your self-will—the very thing you then offer to Christ. But you can't give to him what you don't yet possess. Offering your self-will is an offering of humility—an offering of a broken heart and contrite spirit.

If you are afraid to trust and submit or if you do not know how to begin, go to your Heavenly Father in prayer and ask him to help you plant the seeds of trust and humility and what you need to do to nurture these seeds. Exercising your faith will allow your trust to grow.

> *Humility was given as a gift to me as I admitted to Heavenly Father my weakness and asked for his help. "I cannot do this one alone," I prayed. Each time I knelt on my feeble knees admitting my weakness and my need for his help I released another piece of pride and therefore allowed the gift of humility to enter my being. I can now receive whatever my Father sees that I need. I trust my Heavenly Father—for he is trustworthy. I know he is trustworthy because when I humble myself and return to him daily; he is always there for me.*
>
> *—A Survivor*

But that ye would humble yourselves before the Lord, and call on his holy name, and watch and pray continually, that ye may not be tempted above that which ye can bear, and thus be led by the Holy Spirit, becoming humble, meek, submissive, patient, full of love and all long-suffering. (Alma 13:28.)

Please keep in mind that this experience of trusting and submitting is a process that takes time. Give yourself time to learn to trust and submit to God. The blessings of trusting and submitting to God are immeasurable in aiding you on your path to wholeness. God is waiting to help you heal.

1. Francine Bennion, "A Latter-day Saint Theology of Suffering," *A Heritage of Faith*. Salt Lake City, Utah: Deseret Book, 1988, p. 66.

2. "The Uses of Adversity," *Women of Faith*. Salt Lake City, Utah: Deseret Book, 1989, p. 173.

3. "I Have A Question," *Ensign*, August 1986, p.38.

4. Dennis Rasmussen, *The Lord's Question*. American Fork, Utah: Covenant Communications, Inc., 1985, pp. 63-64.

5. "It Takes More Than Love," *Ensign*, August, 1990, p.19.

6. *Time*, February 5, 1973, p. 35.

7. Richard G. Scott, "Healing the Scars of Abuse," *Ensign*, May, 1992, p. 32.

8. Ann N. Madsen, "A Voice Demands That We Ascend," *Women of Faith*. Salt Lake City, Utah: Deseret Book, 1989, p. 162.

9. Julie Rochelle-Stevens, *In Reflection*, monthly newsletter, (Portland, Oregon: December 1991,) Vol. 1, N. 9, p.4

10. "Unrighteous Dominion," *Ensign*, July, 1989, p. 9.

11. Desktop Franklin Master Dictionary

# CHAPTER 8
## FORGIVING WHEN IT'S TIME

*Forgive?*
*Will I forgive, you cry.*
*But*
*What is the Gift,*
*The favor?*
*You would lift*
*Me from*
*My poor place*
*To stand beside*
*The Savior.*
*You would have*
*Me see with*
*His eyes,*
*Smile, And with Him*
*Reach out to*

*Salve*
*A sorrowing*
*heart—*
*For one small*
*Moment*
*To Share in*
*Christ's great art.*

*Will I forgive,*
*You cry.*
*Oh,*
*May I—*
*May I?*
　　　　*—Carol Lynn*
　　　　　　*Pearson[1]*

*M*uch counsel and advice that may be appropriate for other experiences necessitating forgiveness are not appropriate for the experiences of incest and childhood sexual abuse. I was harmed during early childhood in a way that hurt me deeply, leaving profound spiritual scars. This abuse harmed me so deeply that for many years I was not able to perceive life in a way that allowed me to heal. I had, in effect, worn "dark glasses" over my masks of abuse all these years so that I could survive the pain.

Part of healing is clearing up your misconceptions about forgiveness. We will discuss four myths about forgiveness and abuse, the forgiveness process, the stages involved, and some answers to questions about forgiveness as it relates to healing from incest and child sexual abuse. I hope this information will help facilitate your experience of forgiveness in your own recovery process.

## Myths about Forgiveness and Sexual Abuse

I believe there are four myths commonly associated with forgiveness and healing from childhood sexual abuse and incest:
1. The survivor needs to seek forgiveness.
2. The survivor should forgive and forget.
3. Reconciliation is the goal of forgiveness.
4. It is better for the survivor if forgiveness comes quickly, early in the process of healing.

These myths, in a variety of ways, are frequently given as counsel by well-meaning people to survivors during the recovery process. If believed, they can be very damaging to the survivor. Encouraging premature forgiveness violates the healing process by pushing survivors into a stage of recovery they are not ready to deal with.

## Myth 1: The survivor needs to seek forgiveness.

If you were sexually abused as a child, you DO NOT need to seek forgiveness for that abuse—ever. As a child victim, I was completely innocent—I did nothing to cause the abuse. And neither did you. You are not responsible for that sin. Your abuser is responsible and is the one who needs to seek forgiveness.

As the survivor of the abuse, you should recognize that

you have been horribly wronged and that you must heal from your abuse before you can forgive the one who has wronged you. True forgiveness can come only when you have healed and have therefore become emotionally, psychologically, and spiritually strong and capable of forgiving your abuser.

If you have felt the need to seek forgiveness in order to get rid of your feelings of shame and powerlessness, you are not alone. Many survivors have been told that they were to blame for their abuse. Some survivors feel responsible because they were unable to protect themselves. Remember: The blame for the child sexual abuse (including incest) inflicted upon you must be put where it belongs—on the person or persons who abused you.

Until you have healed, you are not totally free from the generational sins of your parents or the sins of the perpetrator. The sins they inflicted on you have wounded you in a way that has affected your entire life. As a result of such an unhealed wound, some survivors become perpetrators who must heal from the abuse inflicted on them before they can overcome their own need to abuse. Other survivors may commit other sins until they heal. It is unhealed wounds that gives Satan power over abusers. As a result of the abuse you suffered as a child, you may have internalized all kinds of unhealthy behaviors in your effort to survive. Forgiveness for any residual effects this abuse may have had in your life is the only forgiveness you need to seek.

You must also forgive yourself for the limitations you've lived with as an adult. You must forgive yourself for repeating your victimization, for not knowing how to protect your own children, or for abusing others. You must forgive yourself for needing time to heal now, and you must give yourself, as generously as you can, all your compassion and understanding, so you can direct your attention and energy toward your own healing. This forgiveness is what's essential.[2]

*Forgiveness of self is where all forgiveness begins. If I am unable to forgive myself it is impossible for me to forgive others. I cannot give what I do not have. I need to forgive myself for being so needy and choosing to take care of my neediness in inappropriate ways. Repenting and forgiving myself for breaking any of God's laws while trying to take care of my neediness is critical before I can even consider forgiving anyone else.*

*Forgiving myself means being able to release myself from unnecessary guilt by having a clear understanding of who is responsible for what actions. It means admitting what is really my own wrongdoing and knowing I didn't make anyone do anything to me when I was a child. Being able to separate clearly what I am responsible for and what wrong-doing others are responsible for is where my self-forgiveness began.*

—*A Survivor*

I never felt like I needed to be forgiven for my abuse. But I have needed to repent and seek forgiveness for the way I hurt my family with my rage and anger. As I have repented and forgiven myself of the residual effects of my abuse, I have experienced a unique healing. Through this healing, it is possible for survivors to gain the ability to love themselves and others with a clarity of spiritual understanding that is amazing. Healing results in a personal peace that will bring you great joy.

## Myth 2: The survivor should forgive and forget.

Survivors are often counseled to forgive and forget. As a result, many survivors try to go directly from suffering to forgiveness—eliminating all the steps of healing in between. Forgiving is not forgetting. It is healing the wounds of your childhood and being able to remember in peace. David Augsburger has written, "When forgiveness denies that there is anger, acts as if it never happened, smiles as though it never hurts, fakes as though it is all forgotten . . . it is not forgiveness. It is a magical fantasy."[3]

Joanne Ross Feldmeth and Midge Wallace Finley add this: "People who confuse this magical fantasy of forgiveness with Christlike forgiveness assume that a person who tells the truth, admits her pain, grieves her losses, and expresses her feelings is involved only in the process of anger and retribution."[4]

The survivor is involved in the process of *healing*. Experiencing these emotions is an important part of the recovery experience; without them, forgiveness can be fleeting. By repressing memories, survivors also repress the pain and shame residue of their abuse. Managing memories and other associated feelings in a non-destructive way (see Chapter 2) is critical to healing the wounds left by the abuser, which then enables the survivor to forgive, to be healed.

## Myth 3: Reconciliation is the goal of forgiveness.

Reconciliation is NOT the goal of forgiveness. Reconciliation requires a mutual agreement that a wrong has occurred and a renewed commitment to a healthy and safe relationship (which is seldom possible with perpetrators of abuse). In the case of incest, your recovery experience must give you the chance to separate yourself from your family psychologically and possibly physically—to become an individual separate from the abuse and the abusive dynamics that may still characterize your family relationships.

Because there is often family denial concerning the abuse, family members can be a risk to your development as a separate individual, especially as an individual who has already begun to reclaim her personal power and agency. Certainly the ideal is for family members to love each other and to maintain healthy relationships. But no matter how earnestly you may desire these relationships, it may not be in your best interest to pursue them while you are recovering. So much is dependent on the choices of the individual family members and their response to you. If your abuser is not a member of your family of origin, the same considerations of reconciliation apply. You need to honor the fact that your recovery should be your priority. You must judge wisely whether attempts to reconcile with your perpetrator would hinder or enhance your healing process.

As a survivor, you need to establish "safe relationships." One harsh reality of this world is that you may be related genetically or by adoption to unsafe individuals, but this does not mean that you are required to have relationships with them. Reconciliation is not the ultimate goal of forgiveness.

Even if reconciliation is achieved, your Inner Child's dreams of a perfect relationship will have to be modified. It is a false expectation to think that the person who hurt you is ever likely to meet your emotional needs. Beware of projecting your needs onto people who are not able to meet them. Study what has happened in your past to get a sense of what you might realistically expect in the future. Learn how you are vulnerable in relationships and then set appropriate boundaries to protect yourself from further victimization.

## Myth 4: It is better for the survivor if forgiveness comes quickly, early in the process of healing.

Survivors of sexual abuse often believe that forgiving the offender will lead to healing and recovery—that forgiveness is the first step toward healing. Susan Forward helps us understand the folly of this: "One of the most dangerous things about forgiveness [too soon] is that it undercuts your ability to let go of your pent-up emotions. How can you acknowledge your anger against an offender whom you've already forgiven? Responsibility can go only one of two places: outward, onto the person who has hurt you, or inward, into yourself. Someone's got to be responsible. So you may forgive your perpetrator and end up hating yourself all the more in exchange."[5]

Survivors may also be motivated to offer forgiveness early in the recovery experience in hopes of avoiding much of the painful work of healing, believing that by forgiving they might find a shortcut to feeling better. But this conscious, intellectual decision is not true forgiveness. Carroll Hofeling Morris puts it this way:

> The temptation to jump into forgiveness can be great, especially when the victim is encouraged to do so by family, friends, and Church leaders.
>
> In an attempt to be helpful they say things like, "Why can't you get on with your life? You're just hurting yourself by not forgiving. Can't you just forgive and forget? Don't you believe the Atonement? Why can't you let it go?" But as one adult child succinctly put it, "Forgiveness has its own agenda, and intellectual forgiveness is not the goal."[6]

The answer to the question, "Does forgiving the offender lead to healing?" is NO. The survivor of childhood sexual abuse and incest will find instead that *healing leads to forgiveness.*

## Coming to Forgiveness is a Process, Not an Event

I have found that for the survivor of child sexual abuse and incest, the ability to forgive is a growth process, not a one-time event. You cannot forgive while you are still suffering. You have to first relieve the wounded Inner Child from the suffering of the past, to help that part of yourself feel secure. When you are emotionally at peace, you will be able to forgive. It is something you cannot rush or force. If you push yourself to forgive, you push yourself back into the dangerous dysfunctional world the Inner Child knows so well, because she will feel that you have put the needs of the perpetrator before your own, which mimics the abuse.

Prayerfully seek to understand how you should relate to the experience of forgiveness in terms of your personal circumstances, and Heavenly Father will give you answers. This survivor's personal record offers welcome insights:

> One day I was talking with the Lord about how frustrated I felt about not yet being able to forgive. I explained that I saw myself as a forgiving person and therefore couldn't understand why this was so hard. I was worried about what the Lord was thinking of me. And worst of all, what if I was stuck here forever?
>
> All of these questions were swept away with the Lord's gentle answer: "Dear daughter, why are you pushing so hard? It will come in its own time."
>
> What a lesson of faith! My sense of urgency had been motivated by fear and worry about where I stood. The Lord blessed me with patience and with his trust. In that moment, I felt the love and peace that is promised in the scriptures, that "perfect love

*casteth out all fear" (Moroni 8:16).*

*The scriptures remind us often of the importance of forgiveness. We sometimes hear it from parents, siblings, or friends. A few of us may even eventually hear it from our perpetrators, who come to us with an apology and perhaps an appeal for forgiveness. Unless we've had time to process to the point where we are ready for this unexpected event, we may find ourselves feeling guilty that we are not able to forgive. In fact, we may feel angry and frustrated that once again, we're being pressed into fitting the abuser's timing and filling his needs.*

*—A Survivor*[7]

It is important for you to understand that in your personal quest, the experience of forgiveness will more than likely come in stages and increments. I believe that you will be able to forgive when you are emotionally ready. Forgiveness is not something you can force yourself to feel because you believe you should. Neither can someone force it on you (see D&C 10:4-5). You can receive counsel, seek instruction, and study and pray to come to forgiveness, but only the Lord can give you the power to forgive when it is time. The experience and its timing are between you and the Lord.

Please note below that I have taken the liberty to answer some frequently asked questions about forgiveness with which survivors frequently struggle:

**Question:** I feel as though forgiving means condoning what the abuser has done. How do I get over that feeling?
**Answer:** Forgiveness is not releasing others from responsibility for their harmful actions or believing their actions were justified. However, it is important to understand what

forgiveness means to you. You may want to write a definition of forgiveness that you are comfortable with. I compiled this definition that was helpful to me:

> Forgiveness emphasizes understanding every
> person's humanness, limitations, and history.
> Forgiveness is self-affirming. It can allow and
> encourage me to accept my own humanity, develop
> compassion toward myself, remove remaining
> self-blame, and release myself from constantly
> experiencing negative feelings toward those who
> have harmed me.

**Question:** Can you feel true forgiveness and still mistrust
the abuser?
**Answer:** Yes. In fact, that is the most common pattern.
Our understanding of forgiveness has often included the
notion that if we forgive someone, we must also trust that
person. Please understand that trusting the person who
abused you is not a result of forgiving that person. In Alma
61:13, we are counseled in these words, "But behold he
doth not command us that we shall subject ourselves to
our enemies, but we should put our trust in him, and he
will deliver us."

Forgiveness and trust are not the same thing. It is
extremely important that you, the survivor, set appropriate
boundaries with your abuser so that you can maintain a
sense of power and safety. You will want to be careful about
informing the abuser of your experience of forgiving him
or her. This may, in fact, not be wise as the perpetrator
does not need to know about the forgiveness. Share your
forgiveness with the Lord.

**Question:** What if the offender is still being extremely
destructive to others? If victims forgive the victimizer,

won't there continue to be more victims?

**Answer:** Forgiveness is not submissiveness, nor does it mean we should continue to be victims. If you are aware of illegal and destructive acts being committed by your offender, contact local authorities (e.g. Child Protective Services, Division of Family Services, or your local police) and report what you know. You have power through these services to intervene, to try and stop current abuse.

If you are still in an abusive situation, don't concern yourself with forgiveness at this point. You must first find help. You must stop the abuse before you can begin to heal or even think about forgiveness. Healing yourself should be your priority. Remember that forgiveness is a by-product of healing, one of the final stages of recovery.

You have the ultimate power over your own healing and recovery experience, and the ability to get away from your offender. Be very cautious about engaging in a private campaign to stop your offender from hurting more people. This could be extremely harmful to you. We live in a world of terrible, unjust acts committed daily. We must have hope in the Lord's consummate plan to bring justice and mercy, in his own time, to those who have committed these horrific acts.

**Question:** What do I do if the offender has asked me for forgiveness and I'm not ready to forgive?

**Answer:** Forgiveness is not true forgiveness if offered prematurely or forced. Realize that your forgiveness is an offering with no time line. The abuser's time line is insignificant. It is important that your forgiveness is on the Lord's time line. Pray and seek inspiration, and protect yourself from your offender. You do not need to respond to verbal requests and pressure that you should be offering forgiveness because the abuser feels ready to receive it. If you feel you must respond, you can simply explain to the abuser that you're not ready to forgive him/her yet.

## Some Closing Thoughts

As with most survivors, during the early stages of my recovery it was difficult for me to grasp why I needed to forgive. Why should I forgive people who have never admitted any wrong doing? Why should I forgive people who are not seeking repentance and forgiveness for their wrong-doing?

I was fortunate not to feel pressured by anyone, including myself, to come to feelings of forgiveness. As a result, I did not worry about forgiving, and I put my energies into becoming empowered and whole. The outcome of concentrating on healing myself is that I have come to forgiveness without actively seeking it. My genuine feelings of forgiveness toward my offenders have come through releasing and healing my anger, my sadness, my grief, and my feelings of powerlessness. I am now able to feel the love of Christ, through which forgiveness comes, because I feel love for myself. I have been given a hidden treasure—the hidden treasure of forgiveness. I am now able to understand the woundedness of those who harmed me. Their choices were wrong, and my forgiveness does not justify their sins. My feelings of forgiveness help me—not them. They elevate me to a higher place—a place of empowerment and purpose. I am grateful that my heart has been filled with sweet forgiving, and that I have been taught tolerance and love. (See Hymn No. 172, second verse, "In Humility Our Savior," *Hymns of The Church of Jesus Christ of Latter-day Saints*).

As you continue to work through your feelings of powerlessness, anger, and grief, you will continue to release the residue of the sin of your abusers. The release of this residue allows a place within you for Christlike love. One characteristic of Christlike love, or the pure love of Christ which we call charity, is the ability to feel and offer forgiveness.

As you advance to the final stages of healing, these feelings of true forgiveness will waft into and out of your heart. As you respond to these new feelings of wholeness and forgiveness by offering Christlike love to others, you release feelings of condemnation and bitterness and allow feelings of wholeness and forgiveness to grow.

As feelings of true forgiveness grow, they are sustained by the light of Christ, which grows brighter and brighter in you. You will find you are in a different place because you are no longer the wounded child. You have done the work of healing which has opened you to your higher self, your spiritual self, which allows you to see the woundedness and victimization of your abusers and the pain of their lives. Through the power of the Holy Ghost you are now able to "forbear another, and forgive another" (Colossians 3:13), and enjoy the sweet peaceful feelings of wholeness of which forgiveness is a part.

A good friend and fellow survivor not only wrote the following, but lives it. She has taught me why I would even want to feel forgiveness—because ultimately being able to feel forgiveness offers me more wholeness in my being. And with that wholeness I am able to live a more abundant and joyous life.

> *Forgiveness, being a gift from God, means the full feelings and power of love have been received. Once feelings of self-love and love of God finally come together internally they can grow, swell, and increase so much that they pour out to others. This gift of love called forgiveness is then available to give to others—even those who have hurt us if it is safe.*
>
> *In order to sustain this gift of love and forgiveness, the work of self-healing and self-nurturing has to*

*continue until death—it never ends. Another way to*
*sustain this gift is to give it. It is true, the more we*
*give the more we receive. The emptiness and power-*
*lessness that we once felt is healed and sustained. We*
*have truly come out of isolation and are finally*
*interconnected with our whole being through Christ,*
*who is our healer.*

—*A Survivor*

Corrie Ten Boom has a lot to teach us in her book *The Hiding Place.* The following experience occurred in wartorn Germany following World War II. Corrie had just finished preaching the "word of God" in a church where she was approached by a former S.S. soldier who had been a guard at the prisoner-of-war camp where she had been contained.

It was at a church service in Munich that I saw him, the former S.S. man who had stood guard at the shower room door in the processing center at Ravensbruck. He was the first of our actual jailers that I had seen since that time. And suddenly it was all there—the roomful of mocking men, the heaps of clothing, Betsie's pain-blanched face.

He came up to me as the church was emptying, beaming and bowing. "How grateful I am for your message, Fraulein," he said, "to think that, as you say, He has washed my sins away!"

His hand was thrust out to shake mine. And I, who had preached so often to the people in Bloemendaal the need to forgive, kept my hand at my side.

Even as the angry, vengeful thoughts boiled through me, I saw the sin of them. Jesus Christ had died for this man; was I going to ask for more? "Lord Jesus," I prayed, "forgive me and help me to forgive him."

I tried to smile, I struggled to raise my hand. I could not. I felt nothing, not the slightest spark of warmth or charity. And so again I breathed a silent prayer. Jesus, I cannot forgive him. Give me Your forgiveness.

As I took his hand the most incredible thing happened. From my shoulder along my arm and through my hand a current seemed to pass from me to him, while into my heart sprang a love for this stranger that almost overwhelmed me.

And so I discovered that it is not on our forgiveness any more than on our goodness that the world's healing hinges, but on his. When he tells us to love our enemies, he gives, along with the command, the love itself.[8]

I believe that Jesus Christ's atonement allows us the healing power to forgive—to have charity, compassion, and benevolence—and it blesses us with his unconditional love.

1. Carol Lynn Pearson, "The Forgiving," *Beginnings.* Provo, Utah: Trilogy Arts, 1967, p.35.
2. Ellen Bass & Laura Davis, *The Courage to Heal.* New York: Harper & Row, 1988, p. 2, p. 154.
3. David Augsburger, *Caring Enough to Forgive/Caring Enough Not to Forgive.* Ventura, California: Regal Books, 1981, Part 2, p.52.
4. Joanne Ross Feldmeth and Midge Wallace Finley, *We Weep For Ourselves and Our Children.* New York: Harper Collins, 1990, Ch. 9, p. 131.

5. Susan Forward, *Toxic Parents*. New York: Bantam Books, 1989, p. 189.

6. Carroll Hofeling Morris, *If the Gospel is True Why do I Hurt So Much?*. Salt Lake City, Utah: Deseret Book, 1991, p.111.

7. Lorraine Janeway, *In Reflection*, monthly newsletter, (Portland, Oregon: July, 1991), Vol. 2, N. 1, p.4).

8. Corrie Ten Boom with John and Elizabeth Sherrill, *The Hiding Place*. Chappaqua, NY: Chosen Books, Inc., 1971.

# CHAPTER 9
## THE GIFT OF THE ATONEMENT: A HEALING BALM

*The blessed news of the gospel is that the Atonement of Jesus Christ can purify us from all uncleanness and sweeten all the bitterness we taste. The Atonement not only pays for our sins, it heals our wounds—the self-inflicted ones and those inflicted from sources beyond our control. The Atonement also completes the process of our learning by perfecting our nature and making us whole. In this way, Christ's Atonement makes us as he is. It is the ultimate source of forgiveness, our perfection, and our peace of mind.[1]*

The power of the atonement of Jesus Christ is real. The power of faith in his atonement is real. As we live by faith in the atonement of Jesus Christ, this faith provides us with the power to heal ourselves. Alma taught, "If thou believest in the redemption of Christ thou canst be healed" (Alma 15:8). Christ's atonement can bless our lives despite the bitterness or the adversity of our past trials.

We need to understand that the power of the atonement is available to us in our lives now; it enables us to endure and overcome all the pains and sufferings of this mortal experience. The atonement has the power to restore every loss, dry every tear, and heal every pain we encounter.

The answers to complete healing and permanent recovery from incest and all types of child sexual, physical, and emotional abuse are found in the Atonement of Jesus Christ. I believe the powers and gifts of the atonement can heal you so completely that you will have the freedom to live the rest of your life as if you had never been abused as a child: "For thou shalt forget the shame of thy youth, and shalt not remember the reproach of thy youth...any more" (3 Nephi 22:4).

Elder Richard G. Scott teaches us that "the laws of your Heavenly Father and the atonement of the Lord have made it possible that you will not be robbed of the opportunities which come to the children of God."[2]

Like the experience of recovery, the power of the atonement works in our lives as an incremental process, line upon line, grace to grace. The atonement is a gift that we must receive, but receiving it is not a passive act. "For what does it profit a [woman] if a gift is bestowed upon [her], and [she] receive not the gift? Behold, [she] rejoices not in that which is given unto [her], neither rejoices in him who is the giver of the gift" (D&C 88:33). To receive more fully the gift of the atonement in my recovery, I had to learn about it, gain a testimony of it, and exercise my faith.

I know that your faith in the power of the atonement can be the most powerful tool in your recovery process. The atonement enables us to replace fear with faith, despair with hope, anger with love, and bitterness with forgiveness.

## Understanding the Atonement

The atonement of Jesus Christ is the essence and core of the gospel. His atonement *is* the gospel. The word gospel means "good news," and one of the most important parts of the "good news" of the atonement comes to us in the form of grace. I believe the power of Christ's divine grace can do more for a survivor of incest and child sexual abuse than any other resource available in the recovery experience. I believe that full and complete recovery is impossible without it.

## The Power of Grace

One of the meanings of grace is "receiving unmerited divine assistance." In the dictionary section of the LDS edition of the King James Bible, under the heading "Grace," we learn this:

> The main idea of the word is divine means of help or strength, given through the bounteous mercy and love of Jesus Christ. It is through the grace of the Lord that individuals, through faith in the atonement of Jesus Christ and repentance of their sins, receive strength and assistance to do good works that they otherwise would not be able to maintain if left to their own means. This grace is an enabling power that allows men and women to lay hold on eternal life and exaltation after they have expended their own best efforts. "It is by grace that we are saved, after all we can do" (2 Nephi 25:23).

As a survivor of sexual abuse, I needed the power of grace to aid me in my recovery because I am an imperfect being, bound by the wounds of my past. The Savior had the power to open my wounds and assist me in my healing because he is infinite and boundless.

Other survivors offer further insight into the power of grace in their healing experience:

*I have come to accept that in striving for recovery and wholeness, there is a point which I cannot go beyond in healing my Inner Child. I cannot completely heal my Inner Child without Christ's help. After all I can do, the atonement kicks in and makes up the measure for the rest.*

*—A Survivor*

*Because Christ suffered for me he gives me the strength to go into my suffering; to feel and heal the wounds of my Inner Child.*

*Through Christ I know I can purge the darkness from my incest wounds by feeling my feelings, grieving my losses, and taking care of the needs of my Inner Child. This will leave a place for the light of Christ to heal me. Christ will sustain me through this painful experience because he knows firsthand the reality of my pain and suffering.*

*Just as Christ went through pain and suffering to become Divine, I must "take up my cross and follow him" (see Matt. 16:24) to come to a state of wholeness. The difference is that when he suffered he suffered alone; when I suffer, I am not alone because Christ is with me.*

*—A Survivor*

As we strive to keep the commandments of God, the atonement releases the forces of grace into our lives. Just as Christ developed and "received grace for grace. . . until he received a fullness" (D&C 93:12-13), we too receive grace for grace. We heal and mature as we turn to Christ and keep his commandments. (See D&C 93:10-20, Moroni 10:32-33.)

Through the grace of Christ, through his divine assistance, you will become empowered, endowed with strength, hope, courage, and other spiritual gifts you specifically need to succeed in your recovery as you walk your path to wholeness. Through the grace of Christ we will be allowed to reenter God's presence endowed with the attributes we have worked so hard to acquire in our diligent efforts to heal.

I believe that the powers of grace helped me survive the abuse in my childhood. I believe that these same powers are available to you, that they will help you to come, in due time, to a full and complete recovery. As you strive to live the gospel of Jesus Christ and obey God's commandments, you too can experience Christ's flowing powers of grace, which will come into your being and work within you, assisting you in your recovery.

I read two books during my recovery that helped me learn about the powers of grace available to me through the atonement. They are Truman G. Madsen's *Christ and the Inner Life* and Bruce Hafen's *The Broken Heart: Applying the Atonement to Life's Experiences.* I also recently become acquainted with a third book that has an exquisite message of love and healing, Steven Cramer's book, *The Arms of His Love.* I recommend these books to you as resources for learning more about Christ's atonement and the powers of grace.

## Spiritual Gifts of the Atonement

As survivors recovering from sexual or other forms of abuse, we face specific and unique spiritual challenges. The Lord has made certain spiritual gifts available that will enable you to overcome these spiritual challenges. The gifts I would like to address in this chapter are the gifts of hope, charity, justice, peace, and joy.

## The Gift of Hope

Hope is the anticipation that things will get better. Feelings of hopelessness are common to a survivor. My feelings of hopelessness were brought on by thoughts like "Will I ever get better? Will these feelings ever go away? Will I ever have control of my emotions and my life again? Will I ever be able to function again? Will I ever be able to feel good about myself?" These thoughts were very real and prevented me from feeling hopeful.

Others may say, "It's all in your head and if you'd just stop thinking those thoughts you'd feel better." But the reality is that refusing to focus on thoughts of abuse will not heal the wounds of incest and child sexual abuse.

Positive thinking was an asset to me only when I was working with other components of my recovery, specifically healing my wounded Inner Child and turning to Christ. Real hope, Christ-given hope, is more then a thought; it is a deep abiding feeling. Christ's hope helped me through my darkest moments and lifted me when I felt I could go no further. This hope in Christ came through my faith, "which maketh an anchor to the souls of [women]" (Ether 12:4).

There may be times when you feel you have lost all hope, that things will not get better and you want to give up. But the mere fact that you don't act on suicidal thoughts, or that you continue to go back to your support group when you say you won't, or that you keep praying when you feel you've been abandoned by God, or that you just keep getting up in the morning—all of these indicate that you still possess some degree of hope.

I believe God will give you hope in your deepest, darkest moments. You may not feel hopeful at the time, but in retrospect you will look back and see that God gave you the gift of hope, the energy to keep trying, the belief somewhere in your soul that things would get better.

During the most painful moments of my recovery I felt hopeless. There were times I wanted to give up, even to the extreme of not wanting to continue living. I never thought of specific ways I might end my life, but I often thought that dying was the only way I could be released from the emotional pain that was engulfing me.

During my deepest moments of darkness and despair I tried to generate enough hope for twenty minutes or a couple of hours; I tried not to worry about coming up with more hope than that. As I look back and reflect on those times I realize now that the gift of hope *was* given to me to keep me alive and working through my most painful issues in order that I might come to the joyful place I am now.

As you progress in your recovery, you will begin to feel "full of hope." This feeling of hope comes to us as a result of our "meekness and lowliness of heart" and is given to us through the power of the "Holy Ghost, which Comforter filleth with hope" (Moroni 8:26). As we "fast and pray oft" we will "wax stronger and stronger" and be "filled with joy and consolation" (Helaman 3:35). The feelings of consolation are feelings of hope. Consolation is the soothing of grief, bringing with it feelings of comfort, cheer, and solace. The light of Christ within you will continue to grow brighter, filling you with feelings of hope as you continue to recover and heal.

## The Gift of Charity

Charity is the "highest, noblest, strongest kind of love, not merely affection; the pure love of Christ."[3] The Book of Mormon testifies that charity never fails; it endures forever. All men and women should have it, for without charity we are nothing. (See Moroni 7:44-47; 2 Nephi 26:30.) In the process of becoming whole, you will begin to experience this kind of love for God, yourself, and your fellow human beings.

I have felt what it means to be filled with charity, the "pure love of Christ." As it says in Moroni 7:48: "Pray unto the Father with all the energy of heart that ye may be filled with this love, which he hath bestowed upon all who are true followers of his son Jesus Christ . . . ."

I felt this love come into my being as a part of my healing through the power of the atonement. I must now pray with all the energy of my heart to keep this love and to know what I must do to retain it and nurture it.

Charity is the highest level of love; it is a gift that takes time to acquire. It comes as a by-product of healing and as a reward for earnest prayer and coming to Christ with a broken heart and a contrite spirit.

During the process of your recovery, love may seem fleeting at times. When love does not flow easily, perhaps the most you can do is decide not to hurt someone. If we each avoided hurting people, lives would be transformed; we'd see the world with a fresh perspective.

In order to sustain love, we have to give love. We can heal one another by loving one another. If you are afraid to open your heart again to receive the love and charity of others, try "passing on" the love of God to others.

## The Gift of Justice

Justice is defined as fairness and a reward or penalty as deserved. As a survivor, I believe that my abusers should receive their just punishment for the damage they have caused in my life and possibly the lives of other victims. Because our experience with justice can be so fleeting and unjust, with very few perpetrators served their just punishment in this life, it is important to examine both the spiritual and temporal forms of justice and what we can expect from each.

## Spiritual (Divine) Justice

As a survivor of incest and child sexual abuse, you could be dealing with feelings of revenge and retribution toward your offender, especially if your offender appears to lead a functional, successful life. This is especially the case if the offender is still in good standing with his or her family and the church.

There is a danger of getting stuck in these feelings, and feeling very justified in them. You have been wronged, but focusing incessantly on bringing justice or reform to the abuser will be counter-productive to your healing. Letting go of these feelings allows you to focus on yourself—the only person you can actually control. By not letting go, you are in a state of focusing on another's actions, thoughts, words, and beliefs—none of which you can control. You must let go and trust in the justice to the Lord. By doing this, you will allow yourself to overcome the powerlessness of trying to change others and to focus on your own healing and recovery.

In a 1992 General Conference Address, Elder Richard G. Scott counseled us:

> not [to] waste effort in revenge or retribution against your aggressor. Focus on your responsibility to do what is in your power to correct. Leave the handling of the offender to civil and church authorities. Whatever they do, eventually the guilty will face the Perfect Judge. Ultimately the unrepentant abuser will be punished by a just and loving God. The purveyors of filth and harmful substances who knowingly incite others to acts of violence and deprivation, and those who promote a climate of permissiveness and corruption, will be sentenced. Predators who victimize the innocent and justify their own corrupted life by enticing others to adopt their depraved ways will be

held accountable. Of such, the Master has warned: "But whoso shall offend one of these little ones which believe in me it were better for him that a millstone were hanged about his neck, and that he were drowned in the depth of the sea" (Matthew 18:6).[4]

Give the power of justice to Him that knows the reality of injustice. As Elder Neal A. Maxwell counsels,

> We cannot counsel him about being misrepresented, misunderstood, or betrayed—or what it is like when even friends falter.
>
> We cannot educate him regarding injustice or compare failures of judicial systems with the Giver of the Law, who, in divine dignity, endured its substantive and procedural perversion.
>
> And when we feel so alone, we cannot presume to teach him, who at the apogee of his agony, trod "the winepress alone," anything about feeling forsaken. (See D&C 76:107; Matt. 27:46.)[5]

We will all stand before the judgment seat of Christ and confess our lives, giving an accounting of ourselves to him. (See Romans 14: 10-13.) Christ has told us to "fear not thine enemies, for they are in mine hands and I will do my pleasure with them" (D&C 136:30). I recommend that you work on your own salvation and sanctification, so that you will be prepared to stand before Christ and receive his blessing: "Well done thou good and faithful servant....enter thou into the joy of the Lord" (Matthew 25:21).

### Temporal (Legal) Justice

It is your right and your responsibility to yourself and others to seek legal action against a perpetrator that is still threatening to abuse you or your children. However, before doing so, seek legal advice from appropriate legal authorities as well as spiritual counsel from a responsible, understanding church leader.

If the offender is a relative or if other extended family members are at risk, you will probably feel responsible to communicate with them and warn them of the danger. This can be problematic for you if there is family denial and lack of support. Before confronting your family, assess your situation carefully to determine the risk.

Remember, your primary concern is to heal yourself. If you choose to confront other family members concerning the perpetrator, be aware of consequences that could be regressive to your healing if you are not ready to face them. After prayerfully making a decision to take legal action, go to those who are in legal authority to pursue protection for yourself and others.

You must remember that prosecuting child sexual abusers is difficult. Social services and judicial systems that intervene can prove inadequate. When brought to trial, penalties are often insufficient.

I have decided the most effective way to stop abuse is to empower the victims and survivors. As long as there are victims, there will be offenders. We must appropriately educate our children to the reality and threat of sexual abuse in their lives. We must teach them how to protect themselves and how to say "NO."

Even when we have done all within our power to prevent abuse, it may still happen. When it does, we must allow victims to talk about their abuse and seek help early. We must hope for and help create better laws to protect our children and families. When sexual abuse occurs within our own families, we must have the faith and courage to confront it, stop it, and heal from it. We can rise above the shame and secrecy of incest and sexual abuse, then be willing to help others do the same.

## The Gifts of Peace and Joy

"Men [and women] are that they might have joy" (2 Nephi 2:25); "in this life I might have joy" (Moses 5:10); "thou mayest know the mysteries and peaceable things—that which bringeth joy" (D&C 42:61); "I will impart unto you my spirit which shall fill your soul with joy" (D&C 11:13).

The above scriptures taught me that one of the outcomes of my mortal existence was to know and feel the joy of genuine peace. Feelings of joy and peace can mean the following to survivors of child sexual abuse and incest:

- To feel innately valuable and worthwhile.
- To feel you have choices and the power to make wise decisions.
- To feel the beauty of your body.
- To want to take care of yourself, because you love yourself.
- To feel there is nowhere you have to go and nothing you have to do. (I really did accomplish this feeling as I learned to make it a priority to take care of myself! It is possible for you, too.)
- To feel the love of Heavenly Father and his son Jesus Christ.

As you continue to heal your wounds of incest and child sexual abuse I pray that you, too, will experience feelings of emotional joy as profoundly as you have experienced emotional pain. Alma said it this way:

> O Jesus, thou son of God, have mercy on me,
> who am in the gall of bitterness, and am encircled
> about by the everlasting chains of death. And

now, behold, when I thought this, I could remember my pains no more; . . . and oh, what joy, and what marvelous light I did behold; yea, my soul was filled with joy as exceeding as was my pain! (Alma 36:19-19.)

I have come to understand that recovery does not mean a constant state of peace and joy. Some days I feel like a nine on a recovery scale of one to ten—ten being fully recovered. Then, other days, I feel like I am only at a three. The difference between where I am now and where I was when I began this work is that I now know who I am, what I need to do to take care of myself, and that I have a *right* to take care of myself. As a result my down times do not last more then a few hours and are becoming more and more infrequent. At level nine I experience regular, but not constant, genuine and pure feelings of peace and joy. I feel the peace and joy that comes from loving myself again and knowing I have the power to make choices and set boundaries that come from my wholeness and not my woundedness. True peace and joy come from a loving Heavenly Father and Savior. They come from loving and serving my family and friends. And most importantly, they come from knowing that I am innately valuable just because I exist!

Another survivor shares her feelings:

*Life is not necessarily easier, but it is better now. Chains have been broken that bound my progression. New chains are visible and the cycle continues. With each chain that is broken comes a lightness and an added feeling of freedom. I truly believe that as I wait upon the Lord my strength will be renewed, and I shall mount up with wings as eagles and I shall run, and not be weary, and walk and not faint, just as the scriptures promise. There is still*

*pain, but now there is a like measure of joy.*
                                    —*A Survivor*[6]

The gifts of joy and peace, along with other spiritual gifts identified in this section are there for the asking. You have some very powerful tools to use in your recovery experience, but they will lay locked and dormant until you seek them out and live worthy to receive them. If you are like most of the survivors I have known, you are more than worthy to receive these gifts. Any doubt of your own worthiness is a product of your wounded self-esteem. You are not a clear judge of your worthiness when you feel wounded and worthless. Love yourself enough to start using these spiritual gifts in your recovery process, and if you can't quite love yourself enough, do as I did: "Fake it, til you make it."

Remember that God loves you more than you can comprehend and he wants you to receive what he is waiting to offer you—the power to overcome any residual effects you are dealing with as a result of being a victim of childhood abuse. I cannot emphasize this point enough: God loves you and you are worth all he has to offer. Use all of this in your recovery. Remember always: Regardless of your actions, in spite of your weaknesses, you deserve God's love. There are no conditions and nothing you must do to earn it. The love of God, by his very nature of being God, is constant and unchangeable. It is always there for you—no matter what!

## Come unto Christ

Come unto Christ and align your will with God's will. Come unto Christ and become God-reliant as well as self-reliant. Come unto Christ and "build your foundation on the rock of Christ's salvation" (Helaman 5:12). Come unto Christ and "bring forth works of righteousness" (Alma 5:

33-36). "Behold, he sendeth an invitation unto all men [and women], for the arms of mercy are extended towards them . . . . Yea, he saith: Come unto me and ye shall partake of the fruit of the tree of life" (Alma 5:33-34).

> Recognize that you are a beloved child of your Heavenly Father. He loves you perfectly and can help you as no earthly parent, spouse, or devoted friend can. His Son gave his life so that by faith in him and obedience to his teachings you can be made whole. He is the consummate healer.
>
> Gain trust in the love and compassion of your elder brother, Jesus Christ, by pondering the scriptures. As with the Nephites, he tells you, "I have compassion upon you; my bowels are filled with mercy . . . I see that your faith is sufficient that I should heal you" (3 Nephi 17:7-8).[7]

Turn to the Savior in your healing. I bear testimony that there is no greater source of help than in "coming unto Christ." He will show you the way. Through his influence, you will be able to make choices that will be in your best interest. He will give you strength and courage to change your life, so that you may bring yourself to a new life—one filled with love, peace, and joy.

As I recovered from my abuse, the blessings that came to me as I strove to "come unto Christ" were wonderfully fulfilling. Wrapped in the Savior's love I became as secure as a newborn child. But added to me, as a result of healing my woundedness, were knowledge, experience, and freedom of choice to guide me and make me strong.

I am grateful for the power of God made available to me through my faith and humility, which has sweetened the bitterness of my life; for the Atonement of Jesus Christ and its healing power; for the gift of hope given to me through the Savior, which kept me going when I thought I could go no more; for the power of prayer and the influence of the Holy Ghost, a gift that's helped me as I've made difficult decisions in my life.

I love my Heavenly Father and his son Jesus Christ. My Heavenly Father has guided me in my path to healing. The Savior has applied the healing balm. My counselor, my support group, and books have also helped tremendously. But I found my greatest healing agent when I turned to my Lord and Savior Jesus Christ through prayer, meditation, and scripture study. I am thankful for the power of the priesthood and for a husband that has stood by me, blessing my life and our children's lives. I "rejoice in Christ" (2 Nephi 25:26), and continue to "feast upon his love" (Jacob 3:2). In my recovery experience I feel as Nephi of the Book of Mormon did, "I know in whom I have trusted. My God has been my support" (2 Nephi 4:19-20).

I have had to make some painful and difficult decisions as a result of healing from sexual abuse, but I bear witness of God's hand and influence in my life every step of the way. I am thankful to be where I am and pray that those of you who read this book who find yourselves in need of healing will choose to walk your path to wholeness, "coming unto Christ" along the way. You can experience, as I have, the exquisite "peace of God, which passeth all understanding" (Philippians 4:7).

—Carol Tuttle, A Survivor

# EPILOGUE

*A*s I look back, the greatest challenge of my recovery was the timing. During the first stages of my
recovery, I was overcome by trying to meet the needs of
four very small children, and heal the wounds of my very
painful childhood—all this while my husband worked full
time and went to graduate school at night. I often shook
my fist at heaven and demanded to know why I had to go
through this when I had little children to take care of. But
my children served a purpose in the timing. They were the
one thing I was willing to go to hell and back for (and it
felt like I did many times!)—they deserved better than
what I experienced and I was determined to offer them a
healthy childhood. My husband and I are now more capable in succeeding in that challenge and it has been worth
all the work.

As a result of the residual effects of my child abuse, our
marriage has suffered greatly. There were many times my
husband and I almost gave up on our marriage. The one
thing that kept us trying was the commitment we both had
to our children—neither one of us was willing to live without them. Also, we both knew that we would have trials
and conflicts no matter who else we had relationships with.
So we kept trying to work out our problems with each
other. Because we have both been willing to look at our
own issues with a willingness to change, we have succeeded

in staying together. As a result of our commitment and our joint willingness to learn and change, our marriage is now thriving.

How is life different for us now? As a family, we have learned to communicate openly and honestly. Our children are free to express their full range of emotions appropriately. We speak appropriately and frequently about the threat of sexual abuse in their lives. We are very careful to allow them the opportunity to share with us any abusive experiences they may have had, by asking them questions like: "Has any one touched you where it felt bad? Has anyone done something to you and told you not to tell anyone? Have you felt scared by something someone else said or did to you?" We also teach them that if anyone tries to hurt them they have a right to tell them to stop and to get help. I am grateful for the insights I have developed for protecting my children in a world full of risk.

I have learned to appreciate the tender moments of life, to take the time to hold my children, no matter their age, and to validate and affirm their wholeness. I have learned to let go of my perfectionism and my need to do so much perfectly. I now choose to do what I want to do instead of doing what I feel I have to. I now experience motherhood as a relationship with my children—not in reference to my ironing, cleaning, or other domestic duties. I am grateful I have learned to take time to care for me, because without me, I have nothing. I know I can't save the world, but I can save me and things I cherish most—my relationships with my husband and children.

Through this experience I am grateful I have chosen to stay active in my faith and church commitments. I have experienced painful treatment by some others of my faith because of my choice to speak out on this issue. But because of my faith in God and Christ I have been able to see the true source of my faith which has helped sustain me in the face of inappropriate actions and words of others. I believe in my church and its members; there have been and continue to be many blessings from my membership.

"Life is difficult" are the first three words in the book *The Road Less Traveled,* by Scott Peck. Life has been difficult—it has brought me to the very edge—pushed me off, forced me to learn to fly or die. And so, I have learned to fly on the wings of empowerment. I know life is difficult, but knowing and accepting this reality has brought peace through predictability. I expect it to be hard, but I no longer expect it to be joyless. I know more fully the purpose of my life, and I now want to help others find and own their purpose.

I know you have the power to start healing your life. Don't wait for someone else to give you permission. Give yourself permission because you are worth it. May God bless you in your journey along your "Path to Wholeness."

# APPENDIX

APPENDIX

# RECOVERY RESOURCES

# SEMINARS AND WORKSHOPS

Dear Reader,

I hope that the sharing of my experience and my insights on recovery have encouraged you to continue to overcome your own challenges. My husband Jon and I have devoted our lives to helping individuals and families heal. This book is evidence of our efforts. For your information we also provide the following services:

• Speaking to civic groups, church groups, women's groups, and professional associations

• Seminars, workshops, retreats

• Recovery consulting

• Newsletters

Because I care about you, I would like to hear from you in writing. I will read your letters, but because I am on the road a lot, I cannot promise to answer them. If you are interested in being on our mailing list, please write to the address below.

Thank you for your support, and I wish you well on your path to wholeness.

Carol Tuttle
P.O. Box 1275
Sandy, Utah  84091-1275

# ORGANIZATIONS THAT HELP

Adults Molested as Children United (AMACU). Self-Help program for Adults, provides referrals. P.O. Box 952, San Jose, CA 95108. (408) 453-7616

Healing Hearts. Information and referral for survivors of ritual abuse. Resource directory of helping professionals. 1515 Webster St. Oakland, CA 94612.

Incest Awareness Project. IAP is a nonprofit organization with the goals of helping heal the pain of incest and providing public awareness on the issue. Box 8122, Fargo, ND 58109.

Incest Survivors Anonymous (ISA). Provides twelve-step groups across the USA. P.O. Box 5613, Long Beach, CA 90805-0613.

The International Society for the Study of Multiple Personality and Dissociation (ISSMP&D). Membership is open to health and mental health professionals, and to others interested in the study of MPD. 2506 Gross Point Rd., Evanston, IL 60201, (312) 475-7532.

Survivors of Incest Anonymous (SIA). Provides twelve-step groups across the USA. P.O. Box 21817, Baltimore, Maryland 21222-6817.

National Clearinghouse on Child Abuse and Neglect (NCCAN). P.O. Box 1182, Washington, DC 20013.

National Directory of Children, Youth, and Family Services. P.O. Box 1837, Longmont, CO 80502.

National Directory of Hotlines and Crisis Intervention Centers. Covenant House Nineline, 346 W. 17th St., New York, NY 10011.

National Organization for Victims Assistance. 717 D Street, N.W., 2nd floor, Washington, DC 20004.

Voices (Victims of Incest Can Emerge Survivors) in Action, Inc. P.O. Box 148309, Chicago, IL 60614. 1-800-786-4238.

The Program for the Treatment of Self-Injury. Hartgrove Hospital, 520 N. Ridgeway Ave., Chicago, IL 60624.

Parents Anonymous, Inc. Provides self-help support groups across the USA for parents who are overwhelmed and want to learn better parenting skills. It is parent led and professionally facilitated. 520 S. Lafayette Park Place, Suite 316, Los Angeles, CA 90057. (213) 388-6685.

# NEWSLETTERS THAT HELP

Incest Survivor Information Exchange. A national non-profit newsletter published by non-offending survivors. P.O. Box 3399, New Haven, CT 06515.

In-Reflection: A Newsletter for LDS Childhood Victims of Sexual Abuse. For copies or subscriptions write: Chris Low, P.O. Box 25492, Portland, OR 97225.

M.A.L.E. Newsletter for men recovering from incest, sexual, physical, and emotional abuse. Men's Issues Forum, P.O. Box 380181, Denver, CO 80238-1181

Many Voices. Newsletter for incest survivors with MPD and dissociative disorders'. P.O. Box 2639, Cincinnati, OH 45201-2639

MPD Reaching Out. Newsletter for survivors experiencing MPD, deals frequently with ritual abuse. C/O Publication Relations Dept., Royal Ottawa Hospital, 1145 Carling Ave., Ottawa, Ontario, Canada K1Z 7K4.

The Adult Survivor. Newsletter for adult survivors of childhood abuses. 1318 Ridgecrest Circle, Denton, TX 76205-5424.

# BOOKS THAT HELP

Bass, Ellen and Laura Davis. *The Courage to Heal.* New York: Harper and Row, 1988.

—*Beginning to Heal.* New York: HarperPerennial, 1993.

Bloom, Lyn Z., Karen Coburn, and Joan Pearlman. *The New Assertive Woman.* New York: Dell Publishing Company Inc., 1975.

Blume, Sue E. *Secret Survivors: Uncovering Incest and Its After Effects.* New York: Ballatine Books, 1991.

Bradshaw, John. *Healing the Shame that Binds You.* Deerfield Beach, Florida: Health Communications, Inc., 1988.

—*Homecoming, Reclaiming and Championing Your Inner Child.* New York: Bantam Books, 1990.

Cramer, Steven A. *In the Arms of His Love.* American Fork, Utah: Covenant Communications, Inc., 1991.

Davis, Laura. *Allies in Healing.* New York: HarperPerennial, 1991.

—*The Courage to Heal Workbook.* New York: Harper and Row, 1990.

Edwards, Deanna. *Grieving, the Pain and the Promise.* American Fork, Utah: Covenant Communications, Inc., 1989.

Finney, Lynne D. *Reach for the Rainbow: Advanced Healing for Survivors of Sexual Abuse.* New York: Perigree Books, 1990.

Hafen, Bruce C. *The Broken Heart: Applying the Atonement to Life's Experiences.* Salt Lake City, Utah: Deseret Book, 1989.

Horton, Anne L., Kent B. Harrison, and Barry L. Johnson. *Confronting Abuse.* Salt Lake City, Utah: Deseret Book, 1993.

Lerner, Harriet Godhor. *The Dance of Anger, A Woman's Guide to Changing Patterns of Intimate Relationships.* New York: Harper and Row, 1985

Madsen, Truman G. *Christ and the Inner Life.* Salt Lake City, Utah: Bookcraft, 1978.

Maltz, Wendy and Beverly Holman. *Incest and Sexuality: A Guide to Understanding and Healing.* New York: Free Press, 1986.

Maltz, Wendy. *The Sexual Healing Journey, A Guide for Survivors of Sexual Abuse.* New York: Harper Collins, 1992.

Miller, Alice. *For Your Own Good: Hidden Cruelty in Child Rearing and the Roots of Violence.* New York: Farrar, Straus & Giroux, 1983.

—*Drama of the Gifted Child.* New York: Basic Books, 1981.

Peck, Scott. *The Road Less Traveled.* New York: Simon and Schuster, 1978.

*Self-Help Sourcebook.* A national guide to finding and forming self-help groups. The book includes descriptions of over 500 national and model self-help groups, contacts for self-help clearinghouses worldwide, a listing of 100 national toll-free helplines and how-to's for starting self-help groups. Write: Self-Help Clearinghouse, Attn: Sourcebook, St. Clares-Riverside Medical Center, Pocono Road, Denville, NJ 07834.

Walker, L. *The Battered Woman.* New York: Harper and Row, 1979.

Whitfield, Charles. *Healing the Child Within.* Deerfield Beach, Florida: Health Communications, Inc., 1987.

# Suggested Format for a Self-Help Support Group

## Meeting Agenda

**Chairperson calendar sign-ups**

**Group business**

**Opening Prayer** (invited by chairperson)

**Group Purpose** (read by chairperson)

**Introduction** (overview of group procedures and purpose for any new members)

**Sharing by Chairperson**
  Read scripture(s) related to her present point of progress in her healing
  Share a gospel principle studied
  Share experience, strength, hope, and growth

**Group Sharing**
  Individuals who desire may take turns sharing (being sensitive to the need for others to share as well in the allotted meeting time)

**Confidentiality Reminder** (read by Chairperson)

**Closing Prayer** (invited by chairperson).

# Group Purpose (to be read after prayer):

We are a support group of LDS women (or any other religious background) who have formerly felt alone, emotionally, spiritually, physically, or psychologically. We are willing to do the work that will bring us personally closer to the Savior. We are here to connect as sisters and become as one heart with each other and our Heavenly Father. We do this by sharing our real selves, showing unconditional love and acceptance and affirming one another.

We recognize the ultimate power and authority of God the Eternal Father, his son, Jesus Christ, and the Holy Ghost. We have as our aim to study the basic principles of the gospel as outlined in the scriptures, which we believe will lead us to a closer relationship with our Heavenly Father and his son, Jesus Christ, and bring us healing, peace, confidence, and serenity, even in our trials.

We work on our own individual issues taking the necessary steps that will lead us to the personal empowerment we seek to obtain. We do not receive counseling, advice, guidance, or correction from the group. The purpose of this support group is to provide a means of sharing our suffering, growth, and joys in a spiritual atmosphere. Group members study, share, and grow in their own way, line upon line.

We show respect for one another by not interrupting while someone is sharing and by being considerate of personal sharing time. Safety, privacy, and confidentiality are vital to all the members of our support group and essential for the survival and harmony of the group itself. Confidentiality includes not revealing the identities of group members or the disclosure of any personal sharing. This must be respected and supported by any who enter this group.

**A Reminder about Confidentiality** (to be read at close of each meeting):

My efforts to heal and become personally empowered and thereby come unto Christ in this support group rest on the spiritual foundation of my commitment to keep confidentiality. The individual, spiritual truths which are shared here in the presence of the Holy Ghost are sacred. In these meetings the Spirit can bring personal truths to remembrance as we listen to ourselves and to others. I have a sacred obligation to keep their words locked in my heart.

The discussion of personal, confidential matters can cause harm to families and gossip in the church. My presence here today carries with it an unspoken promise to keep silence. I will remind myself daily that I must guard against revealing anything concerning group members. Telling a friend, a spouse, or others in or out of the church is breaking my promise of confidentiality.

# A Husband's Story
# of Support

# A HUSBAND'S STORY
# OF SUPPORT

*M*y name is Jonathan Tuttle and I am the husband of Carol Tuttle, who is a survivor of sexual abuse. I used to be ashamed to admit that my wife was a victim of child sexual abuse, but now I am able to admit that she is a survivor and say that she is making wonderful progress in her recovery. This is my story of support.

I was born into an LDS family that has very strong ties in the LDS heritage. I came from what my father would call "good stock." I was never sure what that meant, but I figured that if there was "good stock" there must also be "bad stock."

I always assumed that the woman I married would come from "good stock." She would be a loving and supportive woman who wanted to raise our children and would be free from sexual promiscuity and drug or alcohol addictions. The thought that she may have been the victim of child sexual abuse never entered my mind.

I was not aware that the problem of child abuse existed in our church, and what little I did know about abuse I figured could only happen to children of alcoholic or drug-addicted parents (who were the "bad stock"). Certainly it couldn't happen in the LDS church, I felt, because we didn't have "bad stock" in our church.

When Carol and I got married I felt I had the world by the tail! I knew I was doing the right thing in choosing a beautiful woman and getting married in the LDS temple for time and all eternity. I fully expected that since we were getting married in the temple our lives would be happy. I believed that as long as we lived God's commandments by being charitable, working hard, giving time to family, church and civic duties, and staying morally clean, we would be kept relatively safe.

Immediately after our marriage Carol became ill and over the next few months she was somewhat hesitant to engage in sexual relations. She didn't seem to be the same person I had dated. As I look back I can see that when we began sexual relations as a married couple, Carol became a different person. (We had chosen not to have sexual relations prior to our marriage.)

Carol often became very angry at simple things such as, my teasing about her hair, scaring her in the dark, or coming up and grabbing her from behind. When I came home late, she reacted with much more intensity than I felt the circumstance warranted. To me these all seemed like little things, and I laughed them off. Not realizing what I was doing, I often repeated these actions, unknowingly driving Carol farther away from me.

Carol's anger and depression gradually became uncontrollable. Sometimes she would throw or break things. I was called home one day to find a broken chair in the kitchen and our young children very frightened and crying in their bedrooms (because "Mom was mad at them"). Carol was curled up in the fetal position, sobbing in a corner of our bedroom.

The pattern became uncontrollable rage followed by a deep depression and guilt for what she had done. I knew Carol understood that what she was doing was wrong, but she seemed powerless to control it. It was as if another person entered her body and had power over her emotions.

Carol also directed her rage at me. She often sobbed, yelled, and verbally abused me over the telephone while I sat at my desk in my office. She would tell me how difficult it was to manage four small children, how unfair it was that I could go to work and escape the children and household duties. I didn't understand what she meant, because her job didn't seem so difficult to me. (As I have become more involved in the parenting, I have come to know how demanding four children can be.) However, when I was home, the kids seemed to behave well enough.

During the worst time of her depression, I was a graduate student and worked full-time, so I was rarely home to help her with our four children who were six and under. Nevertheless, when I was home, I tried to be more helpful with the household duties. I didn't come home, sit down, and watch television. I cooked meals, dressed the children, changed diapers, did the shopping, and helped out in various ways.

Soon, however, I reached a point when I no longer wanted to come home and face her uncontrollable mood swings. I resented her constant phone calls at work. I was embarrassed by her raging temper over the telephone. I was sick and tired of the constant complaints about how terrible her life was and how hard she had it. Our marriage was not fun, and many times I wondered if I could endure it much longer. But my faith in the gospel of Jesus Christ, prayer, our marriage covenants, and the knowledge that somewhere inside this angry, depressed person was the woman I loved was the glue that held us together during the hardest times.

As the months passed, Carol became more hesitant, even resistant, to having sexual relations. When we did have sexual relations it always seemed like she held back her true emotions. Often she would go into a trance-like state and I knew she was not completely there with me.

As lovemaking became more of a threat to her, it became more and more depressing for me. I thought the problem was caused by something I was doing or not doing. Maybe I wasn't nice enough, patient enough, sincere enough, loving enough. Maybe I was asking for too much. I wanted to figure out what was wrong, and help her through it if I could. We tried professional marriage counselors, talked with ecclesiastical leaders, yelled at each other for no reason, even cried, pleading for help—but nothing seemed to help.

It wasn't until about nine and a half years into our marriage that Carol experienced the first memories of her child sexual abuse. She knew there was something terribly wrong in her life and sought to understand where her pain came from. As she studied and prayed she started recalling traumatic episodes of her childhood that had been tucked away in the crevices of her soul.

I remember clearly the day she told me about what she could remember. I felt sick inside, as though someone was twisting my stomach in knots. Carol told me of repeated instances of abuse at the hands of several perpetrators throughout her childhood. I was sickened to think that my beautiful wife had been repeatedly violated in such a way. The thought of my wife's abusers committing these horrid acts filled me with pain and anger.

Later though, I tried to dismiss it because I didn't want to admit it had happened. These things just didn't happen to people I knew, especially my wife! How could anyone do such things?

I had recent contact with one of the perpetrators and he looked so common and innocent. I would have never suspected him. It seemed unreal. As much as I tried to deny that it couldn't have happened to her, I knew it had. Finally, I couldn't deny it any longer; there were too many signs in her life and the perpetrator's life that pointed to the truth.

I found it very difficult dealing with this man, who was a successful and respected man in the community. To learn this information about him was very confusing and difficult for me. I was hurt, saddened, angered, and disgusted, that he would do such a thing. I never confronted him because I was afraid of what I might do to him or myself.

However, on the advice of a counselor I attempted to express my feelings through letters that I wrote, but never sent, to him. I felt better by getting the feelings out although I was angry that the abuser could go on with his life as though nothing had happened.

As painful as it was to realize that Carol had been sexually abused as a small child, it was also a great relief to know that I was not the cause of her pain nor was I inadequate as a husband and father. It began to make sense why she was repulsed by sexual relations. Now we could do something about the problem! Now that Carol's memories had returned and we had found the root cause of most of the pain, I thought that we could now move on with our lives. I didn't realize we were just beginning the journey.

The struggle to deal with the issues that arose throughout Carol's healing process has been very trying on our marriage, our intimate relationship, our family—in fact, every aspect of our relationship.

For example, as the reality of Carol's abuse finally sank in I somehow felt "unclean." I thought that I was the only person with a spouse who had been sexually abused. I felt that people were treating me differently—as if they knew my wife had been molested and we were both "bad stock." At first I didn't know what to do or how to treat her. I was embarrassed to talk to people about our experience because of the "looking good" facade I felt we had to maintain.

One of the greatest challenges I faced was the impact her

child abuse had on our sexual relations. During her discovery period our sexual relations were few and far between. I wanted her to hurry through this so we could have normal sexual relations.

Instead she requested that we refrain from sexual relations for as long as she needed, which was very difficult for me to accept. I had no idea how long I would have to withhold my affections or if we would ever resume a "normal" married life.

Nevertheless, by drawing on the trusting and enduring friendship we shared, I found a deeper love within myself. I was able to say, "Okay, you take the time that is needed. I won't request any sexual relations from you." Gulp! That was a big step.

When I attended a workshop for spouses of abused persons, I learned that I was not alone, that many others were in the same situation I was in. In fact, I found it was very common for victims to ask their spouses to forego sexual relations for a period of time. Unfortunately, many spouses felt if they couldn't have sex as often as they wanted it, that was reason enough to end their relationships. Some supporters even felt it necessary to "fool around" to find sexual fulfillment.

But others described how their relationships were brought closer together, and eventually greatly improved. It helped me to know that there were other victims whose spouses were trying to understand them. It made it a little more tolerable for me, but it also made me very sad to become aware of all the hurt and torn relationships. These sessions helped me realize that it was selfish for me to put my needs ahead of hers.

I also learned that even though Carol may have wanted to have sexual relations with me, her emotions and body responded as though she were being abused again. In her mind I would become the abuser and she the abused. I realized that the more I demanded Carol have sexual relations on my terms the more she resisted me because I mimicked her abuser who gave her no choice in the matter.

I asked myself many times why my wife couldn't just forget about her abuse. After all it happened so long ago—when she was a little child. And I continued to wonder if she would ever be healed—if she would ever allow me to love her again as her husband.

One day I asked Carol "When will you make love to me, to me alone, and not bring in the perpetrators?" Another day I hung a sign around my neck that read "I am not your perpetrators." I did this to remind her I was her husband, not one of her abusers, and she should not see me as one of them.

I see sexual relations as a big issue with married couples because it has such potential to cement a relationship—to develop trust and caring, closeness and intimacy. Child sexual abuse is one of the most damaging acts to a man and woman's eventual marriage relationship because the abused partner is afraid that the abuse will happen again, and at times the victim's spouse feels as though he or she is perpetuating the acts of the abuser.

Carol's struggle to heal herself caused me to look at my own issues. Though, I supposedly came from "good stock" I certainly didn't come from "perfect stock." I had issues of abandonment and low self-esteem that I needed to deal with. I realized that I had to look at my own childhood and work out my own past problems. By doing this I was better equipped to deal with Carol's healing.

I have learned more about myself the last few years than ever before. I learned how to feel my feelings, how to be empathetic and patient. I learned to do visualizations that helped me to heal my own childhood issues. These self-improvement exercises helped me to learn how to rely on God and my Savior Jesus Christ, to help me know how to support Carol, and to deal with my own feelings.

I also realized that for a long time I tended to blame Carol for all of the problems in our relationship and with our children because her anger and rage were so apparent. I now know that I was responsible for part of the pain that we experienced in our relationship. My tendency was to shut down my feelings and numb-out to avoid the pain I felt. I tried to run away from my feelings of inadequacy and self-doubt, but I soon realized I had to face my problems head-on. Carol has learned how to be patient with me as I, too, take the time I needed to heal the wounds of my childhood. This search to better understand myself caused me to turn even more to the Lord for his help and guidance.

In time, Carol and I learned to talk at our deepest gut level, sharing our real pain and vulnerable feelings. I learned not to push for information that she wasn't ready to share. I tried to support her decisions regarding how to deal with her perpetrators. If she didn't wish to see the perpetrators I didn't see them either. Even though her family members didn't agree with what she was doing and her perpetrators denied the abuse, I stood by her. At first, although I never voiced my doubts, I mentally questioned her feelings and insight into her abuse. Still I took her statements at face value and trusted her. As I learned more about the symptoms of a survivor of child sexual abuse I realized that she was correct.

There are still times when we fall back into the same traps that bring out the worst in us. When we do this we look at the process of how we respond to each other in our tone of voice, actions, and words, then we recreate the situation using a different approach. We also try to document the situation and circumstances that led to the outburst of emotion and try to avoid going into our old style of response when another similar situation reoccurs.

I have come to realize that I need to honor Carol's

boundaries and that I have a right to set my own boundaries. There have been times when I had to say, "I'm sorry I can't handle hearing about how bad your life is right now. I have problems too, and I want you to listen to mine for a change," or "I'm sorry I can't handle all of the anger you have and I will not allow you to meet your needs by using me as your sounding board for your misery, anger, guilt, or detachment. If you wish to communicate with me you will need to do so by using creative energy, demonstrating positive negotiations and joy."

There have been times I just had to get away with Carol and go out of town for a few days, away from all of the children and hassles of life. We found that we would relate much better with each other while we were on vacation. There were no situations that reminded her of her childhood and it made it easier for us to be more romantic and have some fun again.

There have been many times that I wished the issue of abuse wasn't a reality in our lives. I have frequently wanted to hurry her healing. I couldn't imagine why it would take so long to heal. Carol reminded me that just because I couldn't see this illness—her woundedness and emotional handicaps, it didn't make them any less real. I came to realize that I had to view the recovery process of her abuse as a sickness and that it would take whatever time it needed to heal.

I am not a professional therapist, though I have been to see many. I am not an educator, though I have been educated. But I am a husband of a woman who has healed a great deal of pain in her life. I am a better person for sticking with Carol through all of our pains and sorrows. Because of our joint willingness to change, our marriage relationship is growing, developing and, maturing into what I originally hoped my marriage should be—something wonderful. Carol and I are able to communicate at a deeper level than ever before. We work professionally together, in our own business, for hours each day. We enjoy each others' company. We have fun together and find happiness in doing many things together. In truth, we have gone through the refining fire and have come out winners. As a result of the healing that Carol has gone through she is a much better person. She is very much the opposite of the depressed, angry woman I used to live with. She is now one of the most energetic, enthusiastic, and fun-loving persons I know.

I have an intense desire to help the supporters who are struggling with how to support their survivor. It is hard enough to go through the experience with an understanding of the issues, let alone without any information. If my experience can help other supporters of survivors be more tolerant, understanding, and give them a desire to endure in their relationships then it will have been worth the risk I've taken in sharing our intimate experience with you.

I could never have been sustained in this effort without the merciful hand of God. There were many times that all I could do was say "God, you are aware of my circumstances, please give me understanding. Help me to know what I need to do to make it through this day." God listened and answered. He gave me the insights and guidance I needed.

—Jon Tuttle, A Survivor's Spouse

# OTHER'S PATHS

*T*he next three stories included in this appendix are by LDS survivors who have shared their reality of abuse that we may learn from the painful experiences of their lives and learn to recognize various patterns of recovery. Each of the authors are very active in their faith and have no desire to blame or ridicule their church. Abuse did not happen because of their religious affiliation; it happened in spite of it. Only by taking an honest look at abuse within religious systems can we begin to stop it.

These stories have been written using pseudonyms with identifiable information about the authors changed. This was actually a disappointment to the authors of these stories because they have worked so hard to rediscover their real selves. To find their truth and not be able to share it with their name creates feelings of more inner conflict as it feeds into feelings of shame and secrecy that they have worked so hard to heal.

However, legally we are not free to publish the authors' stories with their real names if their abuser and other family members are alive and identifiable. Still, the necessary anonymity perpetuates the very shame and secrecy we need to end.

We must be willing to recognize that abuse occurs too often within religious families and systems and then have the courage to change it. Abuse can only be healed and eventually stopped when we bring it out of the shadows into the light—where it is seen, heard, and confronted. Keeping survivors silent and anonymous continues to protect the abusers rather than the abused. This we need to change.

# HIDDEN MEMORIES

*M*emories can be repressed for years. I know
because not so long ago I was living with a very
fragmented idea of what happened to me as a small child.
At the age when most children started school, began ballet
lessons, and learned to play hop-scotch, I experienced a
trauma that changed my life. The secret that my conscious
mind chose to keep hidden away in an almost inaccessible
place was so full of pain that no part of me wanted to
remember.

My memories from childhood were very limited. I
remembered little other than a few events such as family
vacations until I began to heal my Inner Child.

The process—the true realization and understanding—
didn't actually begin until after I was a grown woman and
had children of my own; it was then my older brother
came to me and told me that when he was fourteen years
of age and I was six, he had forced me into intercourse. I
was stunned! It seemed unbelievable, and yet I knew that
my brother wouldn't make up something like this.

He had attempted to apologize to me twice in years past
and I honestly didn't understand what he was talking
about. I remembered something that I passed off as child-
ish exploration, so I told him it was no big deal. But he
kept telling me that it was far more than what I remembered. He finally told me he thought he had actually
molested me three times.

After his confession, it took me over a week before I could begin to react emotionally to this information. I found it extremely difficult to believe my brother had actually done something like this to me! As the days passed, the reality of my brother's confession finally hit me and I became troubled.

I began having nightmares. I would wake in the middle of the night, feeling distressed, but not knowing what had caused it. I could never recall anything I'd been dreaming about. This happened repeatedly. My stomach hurt most of the time, and I would burst into tears without the slightest provocation.

I tried to evaluate myself in light of this new information and my confusing state of emotions. I knew that I was a product of a solid LDS home. My brother and I had been taught the truths of the gospel since we were children. Our religion was a way of life, not something to be lived when it was convenient. We were taught the scriptures around the dinner table each evening; we said daily and family prayers; family home evening was a weekly event. Our parents not only taught us the gospel but lived its principles to the best of their ability. In fact, my father was a bishop at the time my brother raped me. Certainly as a small child, I had a great deal of confusion over what I was being taught and what I was experiencing.

But as the days passed, I became even more distraught about what my brother had admitted to me. I finally decided that I needed help, and yet I didn't know where to turn.

I went to a nearby bookstore, where I found a book entitled *The Courage to Heal.* The book was very staightforward and from the beginning I was surprised that someone else could describe so clearly the inadequacies I had been feeling for as long as I could remember—the feelings of guilt, shame, worthlessness, and inferiority—feelings I had grown up with. I didn't understand why I had them, but they were very real. The book actually said these feelings had something to do with my childhood abuse. When I read about the long lasting effects abuse leaves in a person's life, I felt totally helpless. My brother's revelation continued to disturb me. I had no peace.

I decided it was time to see my bishop. After sacrament meeting that following Sunday, I found my bishop and told him that I really needed to talk with him. He sensed immediately I was troubled and quickly made time to meet with me. When I had taken a seat in his office, my husband to the side of me, I pulled a picture out of my purse and showed him; it was one of me when I was six years old. I asked him to look closely at this small child, and with tears rolling down my cheeks I told him that my brother had raped me when I was this age.

My wonderful bishop listened to me patiently. When I finished talking, he reacted in a very understanding and compassionate way; he told me he wasn't sure what to do, but that he wanted to help me. He asked me to give him some time and promised to get back with me. He never questioned the validity of my story; I knew he believed me. I honestly don't know what I would have done if he had doubted my story or if he had minimized the impact this experience had on me. I was in so much pain and feeling so very desperate when I went in to see him that to have him show his love and support really comforted me. Still full of pain, but trusting in him, I left his office and went home with my husband.

A little over two hours passed before our bishop knocked on the front door of our home. He came in, sat down with my husband and me, and told me he knew Heavenly Father didn't hold me responsible for what I had been through. He told me he would call Church Social Services and give them a referral so that I could receive therapy. My bishop's wise counsel was truly a blessing from my Father in Heaven.

The following week I met with a counselor and told him about the sexual abuse I experienced as a child. I was able to describe how I had struggled for years with feelings of frustration, shame, and guilt. I told him of the pain I had experienced over and over as I felt rejection and judgement from a family that didn't understand me—including my brother teasing me to the point of tears many times. I can't recall what it was about, but he treated me in a very cruel manner. I had strong feelings of anger and dislike for him during my childhood.

I remembered being especially unhappy at home. Around the age of eight I packed a suitcase so I could run away, then sobbed as I realized I had nowhere to go.

I also wet the bed up until the time I moved out of my parents house at age seventeen. I had a sense of being unsettled and an irritability that seemed to cause hyperactivity. I remembered people asking me why I was that way, which only made me feel worse—more inferior.

Once an art teacher chastised me in front of the class by shouting, "Settle down girl! You're going to end up with a bunch of ulcers!" I was terribly hurt and embarrassed.

When I was a teenager I wanted to ask a social worker in our ward if he would find a foster home where I could live, but I never got the nerve to talk with him. Members of my family were always telling me they couldn't understand why I was different from the rest of them. I honestly felt that Heavenly Father had made a mistake, that I was born into the wrong family.

I had profound feelings of loneliness. I couldn't talk with my mother or father because I felt like they didn't understand me. I was the only one who did anything wrong; no one in my family was on my side. I carried these feelings of inadequacy throughout most of my life; they stopped me from interacting well with others socially. I felt that I wasn't as good as my peers, especially at church. In school, if I had to get up in front of people or speak out in class, I would break out in a sweat and literally tremble. I experienced the same level of fear when I was asked to speak in church. I also had a difficult time with concentration and was easily distracted.

As a child, teenager, and adult I had a very hard time developing friendships. I didn't want to be left alone, but I often felt that I was on the outside looking in, especially during social functions at church. I felt very frustrated because I didn't understand why I couldn't succeed with people. I fouled up major decisions because I felt responsible for the happiness of others, but not my own. I remembered being in situations where I was extremely uncomfortable, my mind screaming that I didn't want to be there, but the words which came out of my mouth were always what I felt the other person expected me to say or wanted to hear. My first marriage failed as a result of my poor judgement. So much was wrong with my life, and I had no answers.

The counselor didn't have any answers either that first day, but the following week he told me to seek forgiveness for my negative feelings about my family. In other words, my family was right and I was wrong. He quoted scriptures and lectured me about living my religion. He told me that I needed to read the scriptures and apply them in my life. I left the counseling session feeling terrible about myself and knowing that I would never go back to him.

The experience bothered me so much that I didn't pay for those two sessions for almost a year. I still believe that no one should be forced to pay for toxic therapy.

I returned to my bishop who told me about a twelve-week therapy group for survivors of sexual abuse, the AMAC group [Adults Molested as Children]. This group was also affiliated with the Church Social Services, but was held at a different location and facilitated by a therapist. But when I called Social Services I was told that a group was currently in session, and there would be a break of several weeks when it ended. But I needed help NOW! I was very near a real crisis. So I called my family doctor.

Fortunately, my doctor referred me to a clinical psychologist who specialized in sexual abuse. I told her my story. She was very caring and supportive, and although she was not LDS, I felt safe with her. She respected my religion and never tried to question my beliefs. I met with her for three months before I began grieving the losses I experienced as a child that related to my abuse.

During this time a small portion of my memory came back to me, and I remembered my brother climbing into bed with me, saying he wanted to tell me a story. He would begin what sounded like a fairy tale, then he would start touching me. My mind would go blank after that.

I continued to meet with my therapist every Monday for several months. She helped me begin to understand how being raped at such a tender age had affected so much of my life.

When the twelve week group therapy set up by the Church Social Services—the AMAC program—started again, I was there. Every Thursday morning I gathered with fourteen other LDS survivors of sexual abuse, and together we spent two hours sharing our pain and grief. It was very validating to learn that others in the group had suffered similar experiences in their lives, and many of the failures and mistakes in my life were very much like theirs. I began to realize that, like me, most of the sisters in the group found it very difficult to make decisions, let others know how they really felt, and defend themselves.

I was reaching the end of the twelve-week program when I decided to visit the house where I grew up. The man who had purchased this house from my parents still lived there. He recognized me and allowed me to walk through the house. Being able to do this triggered more memories. As I drove back home I was flooded with more specific memories of my brother being in bed with me.

I remembered him telling me I better not tell or I'd be in a lot of trouble. I remembered crying quietly in the dark, feeling very frightened and alone. I couldn't understand what had happened. I only knew that I felt very, very bad.

Again, with the help of my therapist I realized that I had lost these unpleasant memories because I'd hidden them deep within myself; they were too painful to deal with at the time they occurred. I had been caught in the cycles of self-defeating behaviors as a child and lacked the ability to break free.

Looking back, I still didn't understand why I had so many failures while my siblings were successful; they seemed happy and content, free of the stress and problems I had experienced. I was the only one in our family who had ever been divorced. I actually felt like the family failure, and at one point in time thought that I must be retarded. When we had family get togethers I would repeatedly go hoping that in some way I would be able to feel accepted and loved. But I would leave these events very empty inside knowing that once again, I hadn't measured up. One of the reasons I felt excluded was that I was the only adult in the group who had not married in the temple.

Instead I had become pregnant as a teenager and was married at the age of seventeen. I found myself repeatedly being taken advantage of in a number of ways because I didn't have the self-confidence to stand up for myself. I frequently felt my life was out of control.

As my healing work continued, I finally began to understand how being abused at an early age had affected my life. At times, the fact that my abuse had triggered so many problems caused me more pain than I felt I could bear. When I saw small children playing, carefree and happy, I would shed uncontrollable tears. I would actually feel like a small wounded child. How could a loving Heavenly Father have allowed this to happen to me? I felt so abandoned.

I realized that I had already passed many dysfunctional behaviors onto my grown children. I observed them experiencing difficulties trying to make decisions just as I always had. By trying to make their lives easier and "fixing" everything for them, I deprived them of important learning experiences. I was also easily dominated by them, finding it hard to say no. My inconsistencies left them unsure of the rules in our home.

Because my life was so full of dysfunctional behaviors created by what I had been through, my ability to trust in my Heavenly Father had also been severely affected. I realized that as I struggled just to survive, many important teaching opportunities had been lost. How could I teach my children what I had not yet learned to apply in my life? I had repeatedly made poor decisions that had affected my children's lives as well as my own.

I spent hours reading and crying, feeling angry toward my Heavenly Father for allowing this to happen. It was very important for me to be able to tell others just how angry I was! I needed to say it out loud without being condemned for my feelings. When I finally told my therapist about my anger, she just let me talk. This gave me the courage to later talk about my feelings in my survivors' group. I expected to be told that I shouldn't feel that way, but it didn't happen. Again I found that others were struggling with similar feelings.

I was able to begin to examine my feelings, and I realized that buried under this anger were the tender feelings of a small child. I felt abandoned at a very early age because I was taught that Heavenly Father was loving and protecting, and yet he didn't protect me! So as a child I believed that God didn't value me enough to protect me.

As time passed, however, I began to understand that being abused had nothing to do with me being a child of God or my value as a human being. It was simply that I was taken advantage of by someone much bigger and stronger than me who used his free agency in a very wrong way. I gradually realized that while I had many dysfunctional behaviors, I had also developed some worthwhile attributes that helped me survive the intense pain of my abuse.

I learned to be a survivor without the support of my family, since no one in my family could understand why I had so many problems and failures. During the years I was raising my children alone as a single parent, I was forced to become creative in many areas. I did yard work. I learned to repair or rejuvenate many broken items. I took the old upholstery off our couch and chair and used it as a pattern to recover the same furniture. I learned to do minor maintenance work around our house. If I didn't fix things no one would!

Since we often lacked financial resources, I learned to cut many corners. I took a class in auto maintenance and learned to change the oil and spark plugs in my car. I did my best to create a safe environment for my children's growing-up experiences. When I returned to school for my degree, I was able to do so without taking out a student loan.

I didn't understand why all this had to be part of my life, but I realized that as a result, I experienced tremendous growth which helped to change my life in many ways.

Today as I continue on my path of healing, I am grateful that I was given the knowledge of my abuse. I felt locked into a life of failure and frustration before it was revealed to me. I have been able to reach out to family members and find a level of love and support that I never before recognized. As my knowledge level has increased, I have had opportunities to share what I have learned with my parents and siblings.

My younger brother is a doctor, and he has been the most supportive member of my family. I confided in him frequently, heart to heart, throughout my healing process. With his help, others in my family have begun to believe the story of my abuse and realize how it affected my life.

I have also been able to work on some sensitive issues with my older brother. His honesty about what he did to me and his wanting to make amends is quite unusual and very admirable. It has allowed us to do some important work together; we have been able to talk about what happened and how my life was affected. This has helped me to resolve issues, and develop a feeling of peace in my heart.

> Therefore, if ye shall come unto me, or shall desire to come unto me, and rememberest that thy brother hath aught against thee—Go thy way unto thy brother, and first be reconciled to thy brother, and then come unto me with full purpose of heart, and I will receive you. (3 Nephi 12:23-24.)

This scripture has deep personal meaning for me. As I worked on healing my wounds, I grew to better understand my brother, to see him as a child of God and a human being who carries a great deal of his own personal pain. He was molested two times as a young boy by a family friend. A teacher at school tried a third time, but he was able to get away from him. I know these experiences left their marks and contributed to my abuse.

It took me almost two years to forgive my brother. I needed to make sure I understood just how my life was affected by my abuse before I began working on forgiving. If I had forgiven him immediately after he told me what he had done, it would have been meaningless, since at that point I had little or no understanding of the many ways my life had been affected by his actions. I needed to be sure that my forgiveness was not shallow or given because of pressure from others who meant well, who had no idea of the healing process I was moving through.

It is my firm belief the process of healing the Inner Child for any survivor of abuse is a lifetime challenge. I find that when I am overworked or when I don't take care of myself, it is easy to slip back into old patterns of behavior. Most of the time I feel optimistic and confident, but I still struggle with negative thought patterns that take over at times.

Several months ago we had a lesson in Relief Society (the women's auxiliary in the LDS church) on abuse. At the end of the lesson, I stood up and told everyone in the room about my abuse and how my life was affected. As soon as I sat down I wished I hadn't shared this information. A few women came to me right afterward and were concerned and supportive. I found that many others were very distant, and I felt they were avoiding me.

I became very self-conscious about the information I had shared, to the point that I quit attending these meetings altogether for a time. I finally decided it was my own embarrassment which was making me feel uncomfortable. Being able to identify my feelings and understand where they come from has helped me keep my life more in balance. I now try to do things for the right reasons.

This awareness doesn't always prevent me from reacting in unhealthy ways, or from doing or saying the wrong things, but I have a much clearer vision of who I am and where I want to be in this life as well as the next. I have come to understand the significance of Christ's atoning sacrifice in my life.

The atonement "signifies deliverance, through the offering

of a ransom, from the penalty of a broken law" (Mormon Doctrine p. 65).

Yes, a law was broken! I never should have been abused in my childhood. But it happened, and that can never change. I have been angry for the injustices I have suffered in my life. I have grieved for the lost innocence of a little girl who should have been carefree and happy. I have grieved for the lost opportunities throughout my life as a child and an adult. I have also grieved for my inability to be an effective parent.

Through it all, I have become aware of many blessings that I never before recognized. I spent nearly a lifetime feeling guilty, unworthy, and undeserving. Countless times I sat through lessons and talks at church, hearing information about forgiveness and the atonement, all the while feeling that particular gift was available to everyone in the world except me. With therapy and with the support of a caring bishop and a loving husband who remained at my side, I have a new sense of well-being; I find that I'm looking forward to the future. I feel the presence of the Holy Spirit in my life. I know my Heavenly Father loves me.

> ...Behold, the Lord hath redeemed my soul from hell; I have beheld His glory, and I am encircled about eternally in the arms of His love. (2 Nephi 1:15.)

As I continue to increase my knowledge, to study the scriptures, to trust in my Heavenly Father, I find the hope and peace I have never known.

# HEALING MY INNER CHILD

*M*y name is Joy Johnson. I'm a sixty-year-old Latter-day Saint woman. I was born and raised by LDS parents. Both sets of my great grandparents crossed the plains with the Mormon pioneers. However, this does not mean we had no problems.

Although I have no written documentation of this, there are strong indications that emotional and physical abuse has taken place in my family for generations. The abuse is like a cancer; it is one of my family's deep dark secrets that could never be addressed until my memories opened up at age fifty-two when I chose to heal my life.

My parents met while they were teaching school. They married in the LDS Temple and immediately moved to another state to start a new life. I was born during the big depression in 1933.

My father was the oldest of nine children raised in a poor family. A cousin on my father's side is now working through the horrible sexual abuse in her life committed by her father.

My mother was the oldest of six children. Her father was a violent and abusive alcoholic. The children were so frightened of him they would run and hide when he would come home at night; they never knew when they were going to get beaten. In spite of his temple marriage and LDS mission, it is suspected that he had numerous affairs.

My mother's public facade was that of complete and perfect control. But in our home, away from the public eye, she dumped the rage and anger from her past abuse on me and my father. No doubt she had learned her father's rage and used it as a powerful tool of control.

Living with my mother was like walking on eggs. To cope with her rage, I learned how to be a "good girl" because I couldn't stand it when she screamed at me.

As I grew older I did everything she wanted me to do and more, trying to get her to notice and love me, as well as just to keep peace in the family. When my younger brother was born I took on much more responsibility, caring for my brother daily after school, bringing in the laundry, folding and ironing it, and cooking dinner.

When my mother was angry, she blamed it on me. She told me it was my fault that she was so upset—that I made her feel that way because I wasn't responsible enough, I wasn't doing enough, I didn't do anything well enough.

When I was five years old I had my tonsils taken out. I lay in my hospital bed, waiting for my mother to come. I longed to be with her, to have her hold me and soothe my fears. The other children in the room fussed miserably and when my mother came into the room she heard them crying. She consoled the others, then left the room without acknowledging my pain and discomfort. I felt worthless, as if I didn't matter.

In my home I was told (not taught) to serve—to forget yourself and serve others. Besides cleaning the house, I needed to be obedient to my parents, to respect my elders, to honor the Church, to do my homework, to practice the piano and organ, to always do what was right . . . JUST DO IT!

So for most of my life I was doing, doing, doing. I married a Mormon, had children, and served in the Church. I tried to keep a perfect house, raise perfect children, have a perfect marriage, live the gospel principles perfectly, cook perfectly, take the children all the many places they needed to go perfectly, support and obey my husband perfectly, and so on, endlessly. I had to create the perfect life for the perfect family; I was a "human doing" not a "human being."

I kept up this rigorous routine for most of my married life, but I was falling apart. I was in considerable pain, emotionally and physically. A constantly upset stomach caused me to vomit in secret for fifteen years. The doctors diagnosed a perforated ulcer that was at least 25 years old as well as peritonitis. I also suffered with migraine headaches, hypoglycemia, and high blood pressure.

However, these illnesses did not stop me. I had to go on, to keep up that "perfect" image, no matter what the price. If I kept going, if I kept serving the Lord, surely I would feel better, and I would be happy. I had been taught by my mother that all I had to do was live the principles of the gospel "perfectly" to find happiness, and I believed her.

On January 18, 1985, I was involved in a car accident that left me with severe whiplash. Intense pain radiated over my entire body. I went to several doctors and chiropractors seeking relief, but there were no answers—just drugs from the medical doctors, which didn't help.

Still I continued taking the drugs, as much as I dared, all the while praying for answers, pleading with the Lord to help me overcome my health problems. At last I was told through inspiration to get off the drugs and feel my pain, not only the physical pain caused by the car accident but the emotional pain in my life as well.

I started to work on myself, but I found that old habits die hard; it was very difficult. Deep inside I was still in my "human doing" mode. Physically I was so weak I could only do what was absolutely necessary in a day: load and empty the dishwasher, wash and fold two loads of laundry, and get showered and dressed. The rest of the time I was down in bed.

Before the accident I had three church callings: Ward Music Chairman, Ward Choir Director, and Ward Camp Director. I was doing these jobs as "perfectly" as I could, along with the daily challenges of taking care of my family, but I couldn't handle my callings anymore. I could no longer do, do, do all the time.

I knew the only person who could make me well was myself; no other human being in the world had that power. With the Lord's help, I knew the healing had to be done from within. For years several scriptures in St. Mark had held a special place in my heart. Now they really got my attention:

> And a certain woman, which had an issue of blood twelve years,
>
> And had suffered many things of many physicians, and had spent all that she had, and was nothing bettered, but rather grew worse,
>
> When she had heard of Jesus, came in the press behind, and touched his garment. For she said, If I may touch but his clothes, I shall be whole.
>
> And straightway the fountain of her blood was dried up; and she felt in her body that she was healed of that plague.
>
> And Jesus, immediately knowing in himself that virtue had gone out of him, turned him about in the press, and said, Who touched my clothes?
>
> And his disciples said unto him, Thou seest the multitude thronging thee, and sayest thou, Who touched me?
>
> And he looked round about to see her that had done this thing.
>
> But the women fearing and trembling, knowing

what was done in her, came and fell down before him, and told him all the truth.

And he said unto her, Daughter, thy faith hath made thee whole; go in peace and be whole of thy plague. (Mark 5:25-34.)

How was I going to touch the Savior's robe to be healed? How was I going to heal my life?

I read a scripture in Matthew that again touched my wounded spirit:

Come unto me, all ye that labour and are heavy laden, and I will give you rest.

Take my yoke upon you, and learn of me; for I am meek and lowly in heart; and ye shall find rest unto your souls.

For my yoke is easy, and my burden is light. (Matthew 11:28-30.)

I wondered how I was going to come unto Jesus to receive rest, what my burdens were, and how I was going to give those burdens to my Savior? I decided that my survival depended on my finding out.

I began by praying every morning after my husband and two children left for work and school. I would go into my son's bedroom, shut the door, close the drapes, and kneel in prayer beside his bed, asking for the guidance of the Holy Ghost, hoping that I would be led to the truth and reality of my life.

When I finished my prayers, I would lie on the bed and picture myself as I wanted to become. I surrounded myself with nature—leafy trees, grass, a scattering of flowers—to meet with Jesus. As my visualization progressed I was able to see myself as a child being held by Jesus, receiving his love. I actually felt his love permeate my whole being.

I would then see myself as a teenager. I would share my feelings with Jesus. He would talk to me, tell me I was a person of great worth, and that he loved me.

At the end of my visualization I would see myself as a woman full of pain and suffering. Jesus would continue to reassure me of his love; He would lay his hands on me and give me a blessing. I could feel and hear the blessing as I received it.

As my daily visualizations continued, childhood memories began to return to my conscious mind about my relationship with my mother. I lived through my mother's rages, abandonment, disapproval again. No matter how hard I tried, my mother had never been available to me either emotionally or spiritually.

I worked for three years with my Inner Child, to heal my wounds (the emotional abuse I had received from my mother). During this time I was inspired through the gift and power of the Holy Ghost to mother myself, to prove to myself that I was worth something. I gradually realized I had done nothing wrong. It wasn't my fault my mother didn't show her love; I hadn't caused her rages. I didn't need to feel guilty because my mother was out of the home so much with her music and church work; her frustrations were her own doings. As I continued working with my Inner Child, I visualized a heavenly mother who stayed with me, shared her love, and counseled me. This process brought me the most profound healing experience of my entire life. I was able to make my Inner Child happier, take care of my own needs, and free myself from the abuse I had experienced with my earthly mother.

Yet something still wasn't right with my Inner Child; she was hiding something else from me—something dark and secret. I knew this because she had appeared to me many times in my visualizations without arms and with legs bound together. I found a good woman therapist and told her about these images.

The therapist told me that when my Inner Child appeared like this, wounded and restrained, it was symbolic of her powerlessness and helplessness. She advised me to continue with my visualizations, telling me that I needed to find a way to receive an affirmation of my sexuality. I was even more confused.

"How am I going to do this," I asked Heavenly Father in fervent prayer one morning. A picture of my Heavenly Father immediately formed in my mind, almost over-whelming me. "How am I going to have my personal sexu-ality affirmed?" I asked him again.

I visualized him extending his hand and saying, "Let's you and I walk and talk about this."

I began to cry; Through all of my visualization work and prayers, I realized that in my entire life, I'd never had my earthly father ask me to walk and talk with him.

I experienced Heavenly Father explaining to me that the pain I was still feeling from my Inner Child had something to do with my father. So I talked to him about my father. I recalled that when my father was at home, he was usually in his office or garage when my mother raged at me. When he was around, and my mother would start yelling and screaming, he would never help me. Instead, he would walk out of the house.

I received a spiritual communication that my father had done something to me when I was a little girl, and that when I was ready, my Heavenly Father would be there to help me face the pain.

A few weeks later, my memories began coming back to me—flashes of scenes from my childhood, terrible feelings. And I realized I had other losses to grieve.

The first memory I received was while I was walking on the treadmill at my athletic club. A picture of my father swinging me back and forth in the air by my right ankle kept flashing in my mind. That was all I saw.

Later that day, after I'd gone home, I saw my father swinging me back and forth in the air again, then he tossed me on his bed. The scene confused me . . . until the feelings started to come—the fear, anxiety, sweats, heart pounding, aching in the right leg, groin, and hip. As this scene continued to play itself back to me throughout the day, I realized something terrible had happened. I became nauseated, lightheaded, dizzy, and sick all over, but the flashbacks kept coming. The pain increased in my right ankle, leg, groin, and hip.

By three o'clock that afternoon I was really hurting. I went to my bedroom, closed the door, and lay down on my bed, curled in a fetal position. The scene moved faster now. My father was suddenly all over my little body in the heat of sexual passion. I could see myself as a child—helpless and powerless, paralyzed with fear.

I spent two hours with the child of my past, remembering my stolen childhood. When I was able to do so, I got up and called my therapist, who was available to see me right then. The shame was so black, so awful that I could hardly speak. I finally managed to whisper in her ear, there in her consultation room, that my father had sexually abused me. I wept and wept and wept in her arms.

When I was in control of myself, my therapist had me do a visualization before I left that day. I left my wounded Inner Child with Jesus to take care of until I could return to do more work.

I grieved the loss of my childhood for approximately one year. Then one day I went to a John Bradshaw workshop. John spent the entire morning speaking to a group of adults about incest and sexual abuse. By the time he was finished I was ready to affirm my tragedy. I wanted to return to my wounded Inner Child, to where I had left her with Jesus.

John then took me through a visualization where I created an altar upon which to place my Inner Child, so that Jesus could receive her. I wept all the way to the altar. When I placed her on the altar I wept some more. I didn't want to let go of her. She was so small and so wounded that she needed me to take care of her.

I realized that it was time for me to let go of the victimized child of my past and allow Jesus to heal her. I also knew once I left her there I could not take her back; to take her back would impair my healing. I stepped away from the altar and watched Jesus receive her.

As I turned to walk away, I saw in my mind a three-year-old child in the distance, running toward me. She looked vibrant and healthy, and I realized the Savior had taken my wounded Inner Child and given me back a whole child. The knowledge that this was his gift to me—through the gift of the atonement—filled me with joy and peace.

During my recovery I continued going to Sunday services. I sat in the back of the chapel alone, purposely keeping to myself. I would leave the meetings quietly, feeling very alone. No one approached me to ask what I needed or what was wrong. It broke my heart. I needed comfort and understanding from my brothers and sisters in the gospel. Maybe I should have said something, told the bishop that I needed loving, patient friends in my life, but I didn't. (I realize now that other people are not mind-readers and that there is no way they can know our needs if we do not communicate them.)

Then a friend of mine invited me to attend an A.C.A. (Adult Children of Alcoholics) meeting. I loved it. I couldn't believe other people had experienced the same kind of suffering I had. This revelation opened up a whole new world. I felt a strong need to be with these people (adults recovering from some form of physical or mental abuse) so I continued going to the A.C.A. meetings.

After a few months I felt prompted by the Spirit to start our own support group—a group for LDS women. I found four other victimized sisters. We started meeting once a week. This worked better for me because I could bring the gospel of Jesus Christ into our meetings; I could speak freely of the Savior and our Heavenly Father. My progress accelerated; more memories came, more tears, more feelings, but I was not alone. In fact, I learned that I couldn't grieve alone, that sharing my grief helped me relieve much of my suffering. It was part of the healing.

I grieved the loss of my father for two years and the loss of my mother for three years. I never asked more of my Inner Child than she could give. When she wasn't ready to move on, I would leave her with Jesus, or my Heavenly Father because I knew she would always be safe with them. The grieving for my parents was a long-term grief; it took five years for me to come to terms with their abuse, relive the specifics, truly let go of my feelings, and progress to a more Christ-centered life.

I have now been doing Inner Child work for seven years; prayer, meditation, visualization, scripture study, journal writing, personal counseling, and support groups are all tools I have used. It took a combination of all of these things for me to recover, to leave the past behind and move into a place of remembering with peace (a level of forgiveness) where I'm able to serve those who offended me. I am now taking care of my aging parents. My mother is ninety-two and my father is eighty-nine years old. I have not confronted them concerning the abuse because of their age and loss of memory. I am still married, have five children, four in-law children, and four grandchildren.

I have been grieving the loss of my sexuality since my abuse, which is most of my life. It has been just this last year I have been recovering my personal sexuality, embracing it, and enjoying being a woman.

My hope is that my future generations will be better and stronger. I hope they learn that family secrets (child abuse in any form) destroys the spirit of the eternal family and home, and when those secrets are passed on, denying the truth, it continues to destroy the spirit for as long as the deceit is allowed to reign. Knowing the truth about myself, and the truth about my family is part of my hope for exaltation. I have a good relationship with my children and have tried to tell them the truth. I have talked at length with all of them and feel that they are a stronger generation—more honest, and more free. Through this healing work, I pray that we may again be with our Savior and enjoy the great blessings of his atoning sacrifice.

And they that shall be of thee shall build the old waste places: thou shalt raise up the foundations of many generations; and thou shalt be called, The repairer of the breach, the restorer of paths to dwell in.  (Isaiah 58:12.)

# A Mother's Anguish

My story began eleven years after my husband and I had been married in the LDS Temple. Out of our nine children, three came into our family by natural means, the other six were adopted.

Two of our adopted children came to us as babies. The rest varied in ages from early adolescence to teen. We adopted Russ, our eldest child, when he was twelve. He and three of our adopted children had lived in several different foster homes. All of them had lived with families where adoption breakdowns had occurred, and they had had multiple placements in temporary homes.

These children brought with them considerable emotional and mental baggage, which in turn brought many challenges to us as parents and to our family as a whole. These children would ask me how long they were going to be with us or where they were going next on a regular basis. Russ, whose previously adopted mother died of cancer, seemed the hardest child to reach. His adopted father had returned him to the state and he doubted our intentions to keep him.

It was the first weekend after New Year's of 1990. My mother had been very ill for several months so I had flown out to be with her while she underwent extensive tests in the hospital. After four exhausting days, my last evening before returning home, we were finally told what was wrong with her, and that all of her symptoms could be treated with proper medication. I was feeling very relieved.

When the phone rang, I answered it. My husband, Mike, greeted me, then asked how everything was going. I recognized a certain tone in Mike's voice. I could tell that something was wrong. Two years previously, I had discovered that Mike had been involved in homosexual relations for six years of our marriage. Although we chose to stay together, it was an agonizing experience, trying to carry on as if our relationship were normal both in public and in private.

But nothing absolutely nothing, prepared me for what Mike said next. He proceeded to tell me that Russ, our eldest child, had sexually abused seven of our children but he was not sure to what extent it had gone on.

Moments of silence passed. I couldn't speak...I was completely numb...I was devastated. I asked him if he would meet me at the airport alone, and we hung up. I've had a lot of long nights in my life, but that night was the longest.

The flight home took only an hour the next day, but it seemed like an eternity. I had so many questions. How was I going to face our children? Mike was there on time to pick me up. When my luggage was in the car and we were on our way home, Mike and I began talking.

We had been having problems with Russ for over a year—skipping school, shoplifting, smoking, drinking, lying, and at times, being physically abusive with our other sons. I had told Mike on several occasions that I felt Russ had something on the other children, that the children acted peculiar around him. I felt Russ was very controlling; he always got his own way with them. At times, the children seemed nervous around him. I thought that perhaps Russ was boasting about his wrong doings to the children, then threatening to beat them if they told me.

Occasionally, I found unexplained bumps and bruises on the boys and on our youngest daughter, Ashley. When I'd asked what happened, they would tell me they had bumped into something or taken a fall. Because of the reoccurring regularity of their symptoms, these stories didn't make sense but I hadn't questioned my children further.

I had shared my feelings with Mike more than once, but his reply was always that Russ was just a "typical teenager." Mike became upset with me if I questioned Russ or the children about Russ's activities, and I grew to detest Mike's words of "typical teenager."

When our "typical teenager" had left home in November of that year, the atmosphere in our home changed drastically. The contention was gone; the children were much more relaxed. One question, however, continued to be asked by them all: "Is Russ ever coming back?"

I recalled the day I flew out to be with my mother, one of my sons had asked me if I honestly thought Russ would return. He seemed quite concerned. Since I was in a hurry, I didn't think anything of his question at the time. I told him that I didn't think Russ would be coming home and let it go at that.

Now I knew why the children had been so concerned. As I rode home with Mike, I tried to prepare myself to ask the questions, and for the responses I dreaded. When I felt that I was finally up to the pain and heartache I knew was unavoidable, I asked Mike how he found out about Russ abusing the children.

Mike explained that he overheard our sons talking about the abuse. One of them had told the rest that if Russ wasn't coming back, it would be safe to tell Mom and Dad because Russ couldn't beat them up anymore. Mike told me repeatedly how sorry he was for not listening to my feelings and concerns about Russ earlier.

As we approached our street, I knew that I couldn't face the children right then and told Mike. I dropped him off at our home and drove away, hoping that none of our children would see me. I needed time to think, to talk to my Heavenly Father, to grieve for lost innocence.

Tears ran down my cheeks steadily as I cried and prayed, and cried some more. More than anything, I felt that I had let my children down. Frightening questions filled my mind: How would my children ever trust anyone again—especially me, their mother? How would they heal? What was I going to do to help them? Did I have the strength and the courage to be there for them, with everything else I was dealing with in my life? In addition to this new trial, the deep hurt from Mike's homosexual activities still burned inside of me.

With those thoughts in mind, I returned home, knowing the time had come for me to face my family.

I was grateful that six-year-old Ashley was asleep. As I spoke with our sons, tears filled their eyes and rolled down their faces in floods. They told me what they could; I didn't ask for more. I felt their shame, fear, the terrible ache and confusion in their hearts and cried again.

How was I ever going to help them? I felt so helpless. I was sure the boys felt like I had deserted them. Perhaps they thought I had known the abuse was taking place in our home, even at times when Mike and I were both present, and had still done nothing.

I struggled for answers. I needed to know what to say to them so they wouldn't blame themselves. I wanted them to know for a certainty that what Russ had forced them to do was not their faults. Never had I felt so inadequate.

I spent an hour talking with my sons, trying to console them, to show them I understood, and reassuring them of my love. Ashley woke up about then, so I took her in my bedroom and closed the door. I sensed that she needed to be alone with me as much I needed to be alone with her. At first, all I did was hold her and cry. She hugged me back, but kept silent, whimpering occasionally.

Eventually, however, she started to talk, to tell me a little of what Russ had done to her, and my heart ached anew. So many conflicting emotions were tearing through me. I tried to do for Ashley what I had done for the boys—assure her she was not to blame in any way.

When the children's partial confessions were over, and they were all safe in bed, I fell to my knees and poured out my soul, pleading with my Heavenly Father to lend me his strength, his understanding, and forgiveness for all that had happened. It was several days before all of the boys told me everything that Russ had done to them. As for Ashley, we didn't discuss details until a day later when she stayed home from school and we were alone together. She told me that Russ had done everything he had done to the boys to her, except that he had also forced her into having inter-course.

The following week continued to be a blur. As my husband is a social worker, he knew that Russ had to be reported to the police. The state Social Services came to our home to do an investigation. I knew that it was required by law, but it hurt to watch the children relive their experiences as each were later questioned in turn by the police.

Still, even though the case workers and officers in charge of the investigations were very helpful and kind, careful not to place any blame my way, my hurt and frustration remained.

The police told me that Russ would have to be formally charged because of the extent of the abuse. But the big blow came when they told me that if Russ didn't plead guilty, that Ashley and two of the boys would have to testify in court. How I prayed that Russ would plead guilty—not just so the children wouldn't have to testify—but so that Russ could receive the help he needed.

When Russ was finally questioned by the police, we

found out that he had been sexually abused in two of the homes he had lived in before coming to live with us. He too had been a victim. No one had known about it because he had kept the terrible secret inside of himself all these years. Perhaps because he was afraid that if prospective parents knew, they wouldn't adopt him.

Russ didn't want to talk much after that. After ninety minutes of intense questioning, he finally admitted to having sexually abused Ashley, but he would not admit to having sexually abused the boys.

The charges were laid. Two weeks later Russ went to court and pled, "Not Guilty." So a trial date was set for November—seven months away.

Life went on, but not as usual. Eight children were at home, and they needed a great deal of healing. I say "eight" because our eldest daughter, a year younger than Russ, was not abused by Russ and knew nothing of what had gone on. Still she was traumatized as well; she felt terribly guilty that the children hadn't talked to her about what was happening or asked for her help.

I also needed some healing to take place in my own life. I was so hurt and angry. Mike and I had offered our home, love, and family life to a boy who had been shoved around for years, and this was the result. But I wasn't just angry at Russ, I was angry at Mike for not believing me when I'd told him something was going on between Russ and the children.

State Social Services arranged for counseling at one of the hospitals in the city; it seemed like the right thing to do. Our case worker seconded my choice, reaffirming the importance of safe therapy for our children. Several sessions were set-up so the therapist could get to know all of us and come to understand where each fit into the family.

However, Mike was neither supportive nor cooperative about involving a therapist. On our third visit, the therapist asked Mike and I if we felt the slightest bit responsible for what had happened. Of course, I started crying (again) and nodded my head. I told him, yes, that I couldn't imagine any parent in my position not feeling guilty. When I was finished, Mike told the therapist that he didn't feel guilty because he hadn't done anything wrong!

When the therapist questioned Mike about his sexual preferences, Mike grew furious. I knew his anger came more from his lack of responsibility regarding what had happened to our children in our home, despite his denial, rather than his former homosexuality. He left that day and never came back to any of the counseling sessions. I felt truly alone.

For the next five months, I took the children to their counseling sessions by myself. Some weeks it involved three different days—a day when the therapist would spend time alone with one of the children, a day when we would meet in small groups, or a day when the therapist would bring us all together. I was absolutely exhausted after each session.

Eventually, as heartbreaking reality triumphed, all of the children's stories came out, and the real healing process began. The rage and anger I felt for Russ remained with me, especially as I sat in the counseling sessions with the children and relived their experiences.

The biggest problem with my counseling was that I felt our therapist couldn't figure out why I would stay in a marriage with a man who was not willing to deal with our problems honestly. More than once, she asked me outright why I did. As nicely as I could, I explained to her that I didn't feel like the two situations were related. I also told her that for her to pursue this particular issue right then was adding stress to my life that I didn't need.

Eventually the children and I reached a point in our recovery process when the therapist felt that she had done everything for all of us she could do, even Ashley, though she still felt like Ashley needed to be seen.

Acting on her advice, I consented to have Ashley's file transferred to the Children's Hospital in our city, as they would be better able to deal with a young girl Ashley's age.

For the next eight months, I took Ashley faithfully to her counseling sessions. In time Ashley's wilted and confused emotions blossomed like a rose. Ashley found herself—my sweet, darling daughter was on the path to wholeness.

Was it really a coincidence that the therapists who worked with my family, only one of whom was LDS, had the utmost respect for Mormons? I don't think so. I thought of the many times I had prayed for help and guidance over the last months, and I knew with a certainty my Heavenly Father had intervened many times, purposely allowing me to have these choice experiences.

As Russ's trial date approached, Ashley continued to receive loving support from friends and family. The day before the trial she was even taken to the courtroom, shown where she would sit. Ashley was asked detailed questions, which she answered to the best of her ability.

Afterwards they told Ashley they were sorry for having to ask her all those questions again, and for making the hurt come back.

My darling little Ashley sat up straight in her chair, looked the prosecutor in the eye and replied, "I'm okay. Heavenly Father told me right here in my heart that I've done nothing wrong, and I'm okay." There was not a dry eye in the room.

But I was afraid for Ashley. I didn't want her to be humiliated. Ashley had been hurting long enough. We all had; it was time to put those experiences behind us. I worried that Ashley might become too emotional, even regress, if questioned in court. What if something went wrong? That night I knelt by the side of my bed, aching in heart and soul, and asked my Heavenly Father for the strength I would need for the trial, but most of all I prayed for Ashley, that she might have the courage to say what she needed to say, and know she would be believed.

The following day when Mike and I appeared in court, Ashley by my side, the police told us that Russ had decided to change his plea to guilty, so the trial never came—truly an answer to my prayers.

As I drove home, I knew there was something I had to do—I hadn't seen Russ since he left our home, nearly eleven months ago. Bitterness and anger still clung to my deepest emotions. Yet I knew that I had to work through these feelings. He was still our son. That night, I took the problem of Russ, our son, to my Father in Heaven.

I woke that morning and knew immediately what I would do. I decided to fast for myself, that I might find the courage to face Russ. Even so, I knew that wasn't enough. I didn't tell anyone about my plans, but after the children left for school, and Mike for work, I called the detention center where Russ was kept. I asked the person responsible if I could come and see my son. I also asked this person not to tell Russ that I was coming.

Relief flooded my senses when I was told that I could come.

I sat in the parking lot outside the detention center for what seemed like ages, reassuring myself I could do what I knew needed to be done. I finally got the nerve to climb out of the car, walk into the detention center, and calmly ask to see Russ. But as I sat in the visiting room waiting for him, I wanted to run.

Then Russ walked in. I stood and walked toward him, and he stopped. I could see his confusion, his pain. Did he really think I hated him? I kept going. It was then Russ must have realized that I wasn't going to turn away, that I was now ready to deal with him, forgive him. I saw the love and sorrow, even shame in his eyes that only a parent can see. We hurried toward each other and embraced, sobbing, releasing our grief. When we were in control again of our emotions, we took turns apologizing for everything that had happened. I apologized for taking so long to face him. I told him that I was sorry; I explained that Mike and I hadn't been aware of his own sexual abuse before he came to our family, because if we had known, we would have got him the proper help. My healing truly started that day.

I can honestly say that I've never prayed and fasted so much in my entire life. I've also never felt so frustrated or inadequate. But through it all, I realized how much the Lord was truly with me and our children.

Priesthood blessings given by my bishop and home teachers took on new meaning; the blessings gave me the peace and assurance I needed to work through the difficult times. I was never told that it would be easy or that everything would be fine, but I was promised I would learn how to cope, to know what to do with the children, and be able to meet their needs.

Mike did not hold a recommend, so trips to the temple were with my mother and with choice friends who were familiar with my family's situation. Once in the temple sweet peace would invade my senses, and I would forget my problems and do the work of the Lord; these experiences were cherished times. Afterwards, my burdens always seemed a little lighter.

The scriptures were a constant source of comfort and knowledge, especially the Book of Mormon. 2 Nephi 31:20, states, "Wherefore, if ye shall press forward, feasting upon the word of Christ, and endure to the end, behold, thus saith the Father: Ye shall have eternal life."

Several times when I thought I could not go on, my Church magazines arrived, and there would be articles written especially for me.

In closing I would like to say, "Yes, all is well." But that wouldn't be true. I can only say, "Yes, MOST is well!" Russ has been in constant trouble with the law and is currently serving time in prison. Mike and I are separated and in the process of getting a divorce. My other eight children are living with me, and I feel (as do others) that they are coping extremely well.

Ashley is an inspiration to many. She repeated grade one and is now in grade three; her achievements are way above average, which I feel adds strength to her recovery. I asked the principal, who was made aware of her circumstances, and my children's teachers to include me in ALL decisions made concerning each of them.

Our family has no more SECRETS in our home, and even though sometimes the truth hurts, we say what needs to be said. I make certain that no one is being forced to do or say anything improper at home, in school, or at play. I've been told the greatest thing Mike and I ever did for the children was to believe them, and not let them feel, in any way, responsible for what happened. How grateful I am for my testimony of the gospel. I often wonder how I would have coped without a knowledge of the atonement.

I know that Heavenly Father has been the major healing factor in all of our lives, especially my Ashley. Even at her young age she has a special relationship with him that my other children don't quite have. I also know that because Ashley never saw me doubt her, our relationship is one of complete trust and understanding; we constantly share our feelings with each other.

Does anyone know what the future holds? I can only say this: I know there will yet be many more challenges with my children, but I also know where my greatest source of strength will come, from my Savior Jesus Christ, and a loving Father in Heaven. I am not alone.

# ABOUT THE AUTHOR

*C*arol Tuttle is a survivor who does more than survive—she lives abundantly! She, and her husband Jon, their four children, and their dog Steve live in Sandy, Utah.

She loves the freedom of the out of doors when she goes mountain biking and camping with her family, but she also loves being pampered on a cruise ship. She enjoys tennis, snow skiing, traveling to warm sunny beaches, and scuba diving.

Carol earned her Bachelor of Science degree at Brigham Young University and garnered an impressive number of achievements such as being named a "Family Leader of Tomorrow," and an "Outstanding Young Woman of America," before settling down to her recovery process.

Now committed to helping other survivors, she is a member of the National Speakers Association and serves on the board of directors for the Utah Speakers Association.

In 1991 Carol founded her most recent company, Total Quality Woman, a training and consulting firm to empower today's women. She has volunteered hundreds of hours as a facilitator of support groups and in coaching survivors of childhood abuse. She calls herself "The Empowerment Coach." Recently she was listed in Who's Who of Rising Young Americans.